EVIL SERIAL KILLERS

PICTURE CREDITS:

Getty Images: 12, 21, 31, 41, 46, 120, 140, 149, 202, 234
Topfoto: 59, 194, 243, 249
Peter Gray: 64, 72 (x2), 90, 96, 106, 156, 164, 207
Alamy: 113, 173, 220
Shutterstock Editorial: 186

This edition published in 2021 by Arcturus Publishing Limited
26/27 Bickels Yard, 151–153 Bermondsey Street,
London SE1 3HA

AD007503UK

Printed in the UK

EVIL SERIAL KILLERS

To Kill and Kill Again

Al Cimino

CONTENTS

CONTENTS

INTRODUCTION

SERIAL KILLERS GET SUCH coverage both in the news and fiction that it is hard to believe that we are not all in imminent danger of slaughter. The FBI estimate that there are between 25 and 50 serial killers at large in the US at any one time – which is shocking enough. But that means there is fewer than one serial killer for every seven million people. The truth is few people kill. We occasionally say we could kill someone, but that is usually hyperbole. Most of us can imagine what it might be like to be driven to a senseless act of violence in an unendurable situation. But to kill once is one thing; to kill over and over again is quite another.

Though some serial killers have claimed more than 100 victims, they are not always telling the truth. The most prolific serial killer in the US is thought to be Samuel Little who boasted that he had killed 93 people, though he has been linked to 61 murders and convicted of just four. In Britain, Bruce George Peter Lee was convicted of 26 counts of manslaughter in 11 arson attacks. In France, Yvan Keller was thought to have killed at least 23, though he claimed 150. Even so, such killers are rare. Perhaps that is what makes them fascinating.

Robert Ressler, the FBI profiler who first coined the term 'serial killer', said that perpetrators often bump up the body count.

'They do tend to inflate their figures,' Ressler said. They are on an ego trip, overestimating their numbers to make themselves more notorious. After serial killers are arrested, they often admit to killings they have no connection to.

'Once they're caught, they feel like it's over,' says Steve Egger, Associate Professor of Criminology at the University of Houston-Clear Lake. 'In many cases, they have the attention that they haven't had in the past.'

Nevertheless, the proven cases are staggering enough. Samuel Little had been arrested 26 times in 11 states for crimes including theft, assault, attempted rape, fraud and attacks on government officials before he turned to murder and is now serving life imprisonment in California. Derrick Todd Lee had been killing people in Louisiana for a decade before he was apprehended. Randall Woodfield travelled along Interstate 5, which runs through Washington, Oregon and California, robbing, raping and killing maybe as many as 44 women and girls, while in England Stephen Port preyed on men he met through gay dating apps. Donald Harvey was one of a number of hospital employees who killed people in his care, while Genene Jones was responsible for the deaths of up to 60 children.

But what drives people who kill and kill again? The more they kill and get away with it, the more they keep wanting to kill, experts say. Murder is addictive, it seems. The other question is: are serial killers evil or are they mad? It is a question that can only be answered in individual cases. There is no general explanation. No matter how hard we study them, it is almost impossible to imagine ourselves in their shoes.

Ressler, who has interviewed dozens of serial killers, including John Wayne Gacy, Jeffrey Dahmer, Charles Manson and Ted Bundy, says that the killings are a rush, usually bringing a sexual high the killers can relive repeatedly through memories.

'I've interviewed people in prison that get glassy-eyed just talking about their crimes because they get stimulated,' Ressler says. 'When the urge comes to people like that, everybody's in danger.'

Though the United States is still seen as the home of serial killing, in India, Surinder Koli and his employer, Moninder Singh Pandher, were charged with kidnapping, raping and killing up to 38 women and children. In the Ukraine 19-year-olds Viktor Sayenko and Igor Suprunyuk were given life sentences for a series of 21 random murders. And in Brazil, Tiago Henrique Gomes da Rocha committed dozens of seemingly pointless murders, earning himself over 600 years of jail time.

Serial killing is a worldwide phenomenon and, as much as criminologists and psychologists have tried to classify them, no two killers are alike. Each one is a unique case study. Sometimes their childhood holds a clue. In other cases, the killer had suffered a head injury that has made some baffling change to their brain. Some believe that they are cleansing the world of sinners and they are going about God's work.

'They don't identify with their victims or feel any sympathy toward them,' says FBI agent John Douglas wrote. 'As they see it, they've been victims all their lives, dominated and controlled by other people. This is their chance to call the shots – to decide who lives or dies and how someone should die.'

Some are educationally subnormal, while others are highly intelligent, making them hard to track down and convict. Most are smart enough to target strangers they have no connection with. A study of 326 US male serial killers between 1800 and 1995 concluded that 87 per cent had killed at least one stranger, and 70 per cent killed only strangers.

The most prolific serial killers also tend to be the most organized. They methodically stalk their victims, looking for the best opportunity to strike when they will not be seen. Then they quickly dump the bodies somewhere remote. In these cases, the police just have to hope that, driven by hubris, they get careless.

Although anyone can be targeted, victims of serial killers tend to be the most vulnerable in society: children, prostitutes and the elderly. Gay men are often at risk too, particularly in times or places where homosexuality is less acceptable. Berkeley psychologist Michael Evans says: 'Homosexuals are an easy population to get access to in some anonymous way.' Chicago Police sergeant Richard Sandberg puts it more succinctly: 'The gays are easy prey.'

Often serial killers who target gays are gay themselves, possibly because societal pressure makes them feel that their homosexuality is unacceptable even to themselves. Other motives include sadism or a lust for power over others. The serial murderer tends to kill not for love, money or revenge, but just for the fun of it – because it makes them feel good.

Once a serial killer has been caught, what should we do with them?

'Forget rehabilitation when it comes to serial killers,' Douglas says. 'They have a different kind of thinking pattern than other people. You can't reprogram a brain like that with counselling. How could any treatment turn around that way of thinking? You basically just have to write them off.'

However, for those reading this book from the safety of their own home, each killer comes with a grisly though compelling tale which will take you into the darkest reaches of the human psyche. But be warned. In the following pages you will be keeping company with some of the most unpleasant individuals that have ever been born. It is easy to dismiss them as monsters, but you'll find they are human beings too, each with a story to tell.

ED KEMPER

The Co-ed Killer

ED KEMPER EARNED THE 'Co-ed Killer' sobriquet for the murder of six young female students in California in the 1970s. However, he began his homicidal career by murdering his grandparents and ended it by murdering his mother and her best friend.

His parents split in 1957, when Kemper was nine. Missing his dad, he became emotional and clingy. Fearing he might become a homosexual, his mother tried toughening up young Ed by making him sleep in the basement with a heavy table over the trapdoor leading to it. A visit from his father put a stop to that, but Ed continued to complain that his mother was 'an alcoholic and constantly bitched and screamed at me'.

Clearly this had an effect on him. He buried alive the family cat, then dug it up, cut off its head and stuck it on the end of a stick, keeping this grisly relic in his bedroom. Asked why he had done it, he said it had transferred its affections to his two sisters and he killed the cat 'to make it mine'. On a visit to New York, he tried to jump off the top of the Empire State Building, but was restrained by an aunt.

At school Kemper was an outcast. He would annoy the other kids by sitting and staring at them. Although he was a big child, he was branded a weakling and a coward, and excluded from their games. His little sister Allyn was upset when he started cutting up her dolls. Soon he began to fantasize about killing people – largely women – cutting them up and keeping their body parts as trophies.

Ed Kemper's sister Allyn was upset when he started cutting up her dolls. Soon he started to fantasize about killing people and keeping their body parts as trophies.

Kemper's mother could not cope with his disturbed behaviour and sent him to live with his dad, who had remarried. When his stepmother found him no easier to handle, his father took him to live with his own parents on their isolated farm in California's Sierra Nevada mountains. There, his grandfather taught him to shoot, but was otherwise dull company. His grandmother was bossy.

'My grandmother thought she had more balls than any man and was constantly emasculating me and my grandfather to prove it,' said Kemper. 'I couldn't please her. It was like being in jail. I became a walking time bomb and I finally blew.'

KEMPER'S FIRST KILLS: A FAMILY AFFAIR

One day, in August 1964, he was going out of the house with his rifle when his grandmother told him not to shoot any birds. He turned and shot her twice in the head. When his grandfather returned from a shopping trip to Fresno, he shot him too.

Kemper was just 15 and did not know what to do next. So, he phoned his mother who told him to call the local sheriff. Kemper told the sheriff that he had killed his grandmother because he wondered what it would feel like to shoot her. He had then shot his grandfather so that he wouldn't have to learn that his wife was dead.

Diagnosed as a paranoid schizophrenic, Kemper was sent to the Atascadero State Hospital, a secure facility for the criminally insane. It specialized in sex offenders and Kemper attended group therapy sessions with rapists. They had been caught because their victims had testified against them. It was better, he soon learned, not to leave the victims alive.

At the age of 20 Kemper was released to a halfway house and complained that he did not get help from his parole officer to help him reintegrate into a society which had changed radically in the five years he had been away. He was still steeped in the Second World War values of his father and the conservative 1950s' ethos concerning discipline and conformity. Now, people his age were taking on the police in civil rights and anti-Vietnam war demonstrations.

'When I got out on the street it was like being on a strange planet,' he said. 'People my age were not talking the same language. I had been living with people older than I was for so long that I was an old fogey.'

He reserved particular contempt for hippies, especially the long-haired young women who hitched rides in cars with strangers.

After three months, Kemper was released into the custody of his mother who was then an administrative assistant at the University of California at Santa Cruz and living in the nearby town of Aptos.

'She was Mrs Wonderful up on the campus, had everything under control,' he said. 'When she comes home, she lets everything down and she's just a pure bitch; busts her butt being super nice at work and comes home at night and is a shit.'

In short, they did not get on any better than they had before.

'She loved me in her way and, despite all the violent screaming and yelling arguments we had, I loved her too,' he said. 'But she had to manage your life... and interfere in your personal affairs.'

She wanted him to go to college and get a degree. He preferred to hang out at local bars, particularly one called the Jury Room that was frequented by off-duty cops. He applied to join the police, but was rejected because, at 206 cm (6 ft 9 in), he was too tall. Instead, he got a job manning a stop-go sign for a state roadworks gang. He bought a motorcycle with his wages but soon crashed it, injuring his head. With the insurance payout, he bought a 1969 Ford Galaxie.

His job gave him the money to move out of his mother's place, along with a good knowledge of the back-country roads which he cruised in his spare time, picking up young female hitchhikers and trying to make himself pleasant and agreeable.

'At first I picked up girls just to talk to them, just to try to get acquainted with people my own age and try to strike up a friendship,' he said.

Soon he began fantasizing about raping the young women he picked up, but was afraid he would get caught. Clearly, he would have to murder them afterwards. This would also satisfy the bloodlust he'd had from childhood.

PLANNING FOR ACTION

Kemper put a great deal of effort into planning his crimes. He had learnt to spot potential victims at a distance so that he did not have to turn back or make any sudden manoeuvres that would draw attention to his car. He already knew that there were more hitchhikers on the roads at weekends and that young women were more likely to get into his car when it was raining. When he had finished with them, he would dump their bodies in some remote spot – he had come across many while working with the road gang.

Kemper decided that nothing must connect him to his victims. He resolved to keep none of their possessions, nor any of the weapons he had used in the commission of the crime. It was also necessary to be in control at all times, so he would never go out on the hunt for prey when he was upset or angry, particularly after a row with his mother. Ultimately, however, he broke all of these rules. Even so, the police had no clue to the identity of the Co-ed Killer until he gave himself up.

KILLING FOR KICKS

Early in 1972, he began buying knives and borrowed a 9 mm Browning automatic from a friend. Then it was time to get out on the road.

His first two victims were 18-year-old Fresno State college co-eds, Mary Ann Pesce and Anita Luchessa, who he picked up on the afternoon of 7 May 1972 with the intention of killing them. When he pulled off into a wooded side road near Alameda, they asked him what he was doing. In reply, he pulled the gun from under his seat.

Intending to take them back to his apartment to rape them, he put Anita in the boot of the car. Meanwhile, Mary Ann was placed in the front passenger's seat with her hands handcuffed behind her back and a plastic bag over her head. When she struggled Kemper panicked and stabbed her, then slit her throat. Then he went around to the back of the car and opened the boot. As Anita got out, he stabbed her repeatedly until she fell back into the boot. He threw the knife in after her. Satisfied they were dead, Kemper's only regret was that he had not raped them first.

Back at his apartment, he photographed and then dismembered their naked bodies. He then had oral sex with Mary Ann's severed head. The remains of their bodies were dumped in the boondocks, though he kept their heads for some time. Later, he would return to Mary Ann's dumping ground.

'Sometimes, afterward, I visited there... to be near her... because I loved her and wanted her,' he said. A few months later, her head was found by hikers and she was identified from dental records. Neither Anita Luchessa's head nor her body was ever found and the trail of the killer soon went cold.

But he was not far away. From the contents of the girls' handbags, he had their addresses and liked to drive past their houses, imagining the grief their families were suffering inside.

Following a motorcycle accident, he broke his arm and had to have a metal plate inserted. During his convalescence, Kemper spent time trying to get his juvenile record deleted. Having a conviction for murder made it difficult to buy a gun.

On 14 September 1972, 15-year-old Aiko Koo was waiting for the bus in University Avenue in Berkeley when a Caucasian male stopped and picked her up. In the car, he pulled a gun. Out in the mountains, he taped Aiko's mouth and pinched her nostrils until she suffocated, then he raped her dead body and put it in the boot.

He stopped for a beer and could not resist opening the boot to gloat over the body.

'I suppose as I was standing there looking, I was doing one of those triumphant things, too, admiring my work and admiring her beauty, and I might say admiring my catch like a fisherman,' he said. 'I just wanted the exaltation over the party. In other words, winning over death. They were dead and I was alive. That was the victory in my case.'

After visiting his mother, he dismembered Aiko in his apartment, dumping her body in the Sierra Nevada mountains. Again, he kept her head for a few days, storing it in the boot even when he went for an assessment by court psychiatrists. For Kemper, cutting off his victims' heads was the best bit.

'I remember it was very exciting,' he said. 'There was actually a sexual thrill... It was kind of an exalted triumphant-type thing, like taking the head of a deer or an elk or something would be to a hunter. I was the hunter and they were the victims.'

THE CO-ED KILLER'S FINAL VICTIMS

After his motorcycle accident Kemper was unable to work, so he returned to live with his mother and to the Jury Room where the cops were discussing the missing girls. On the evening of 7 January 1973, he drove up to the Santa Cruz campus, where he picked up 19-year-old Cindy Schall and pulled a gun on her. Forcing her into the boot, he shot her in the head.

His mother was out when Kemper got home, so he hid Cindy's body in a cupboard in his bedroom. In the morning, when his mother had gone to work, he sexually assaulted Cindy's corpse then dismembered it in the bathroom. Leaving the head in his closet, he put the other body parts in bin bags and threw them over a cliff in Monterey. The next day, one of the bags washed ashore and enough of Cindy's body was recovered for her to be identified – or so Kemper learnt in the Jury Room. In panic, he dug the bullet out of Cindy's head and buried her head in the garden.

On 8 January 1973, he had a row with his mother. Fuming, he returned to Santa Cruz campus where he picked up 24-year-old Rosalind Thorpe and 23-year-old Alice Liu. While driving, he pulled a gun and shot both of them. He drove home with their bodies in the boot. After his mother had gone to bed, he cut off their heads, then raped Alice Liu's headless corpse. Their bodies were dumped in a canyon in northern California.

From the cops in the Jury Room, he learnt that a full-scale hunt was on. Knowing that he was bound to get caught, he decided to spare his mother the guilt and shame. In the early morning of 21 April 1973, Kemper crept into her bedroom and slit her throat. He cut off her head and raped her headless corpse. Then he cut out her larynx and shoved it down the garbage disposal unit.

'It seemed appropriate,' he said, 'as much as she'd bitched and screamed and yelled at me over so many years.'

He decided to tell her work colleagues that his mother had gone away. To make this more plausible, he made out that she had gone with her friend Sally Hallett, who he had already murdered as part of his cover story. Then he got into his car and made a run for it. But when he reached the town of Pueblo, Colorado, Kemper realized that flight was futile. Stopping at a phone booth, he called the police and confessed. They thought it was a crank call at first, until he got through to a cop he knew from the Jury Room.

In custody, Kemper made a full confession. The public defender's insanity plea was rejected by the jury, who found him guilty on eight counts of murder on 8 November 1973. Ed Kemper was sentenced to life imprisonment with no possibility of parole.

JOHN WAYNE GACY

The Killer Clown

TWENTY-FIVE-YEAR-OLD JOHN WAYNE GACY was a married man with two children and was an upstanding member of the Junior Chamber of Commerce in Waterloo, Iowa when, in 1968, he lured a 15-year-old boy into the back room of the Kentucky Fried Chicken outlet he was running. He handcuffed the boy and tried to bribe him into performing oral sex. When the youth refused, Gacy attempted to penetrate him anally, but his victim escaped.

The young man reported Gacy to the police and he was arrested. While awaiting trial, another youngster came forward with a similar accusation. Pleading guilty to sodomy, Gacy expected a suspended sentence. Instead, he was sentenced to ten years' imprisonment and his wife divorced him. A model prisoner, he was released after 18 months. He moved back to Chicago, his hometown, where he lived with his widowed mother.

Gacy had had a troubled childhood in the Windy City. His father had been an abusive alcoholic who beat his wife and assaulted his children. On one occasion, Gacy's father struck him over the head with a broomstick, knocking him unconscious. At the age of 11, he was hit on the head by a swing, which caused a blood clot on his brain, though this was not diagnosed until he was 16. Gacy's father also beat him with a razor strop when he was caught fondling a girl. Nevertheless, he remained fond of his father, though he never managed to become close to him.

A congenital heart condition meant that Gacy could not play sports with other children. He was labelled a sissy and told he would probably 'grow up queer'. Later, when he realized that he was attracted to men, he was thrown into turmoil over his sexuality. His heart condition also meant that he put on a lot of weight.

Dropping out of school, he went to Las Vegas where he worked as a janitor in a funeral parlour. Returning to Chicago, he went to business school and immersed himself in community work. Then, in 1964, he married Marlynn Myers, whose parents owned a string of Kentucky Fried Chicken outlets in Waterloo and his father-in-law offered him the position of manager in one of them. His wife petitioned for divorce in 1968 after a succession of unseemly incidents and assaults.

TAKING WHAT HE WANTED BY FORCE

Within a year of his release, Gacy had picked up another youth and tried to force him to have sex. He was arrested, but the case was dropped when the boy did not turn up at court. The police had not informed the authorities in Iowa of his arrest, so he was discharged from his parole there, too. His mother helped him to buy a house in the suburb of Des Plaines, where he remarried in 1972 and set up a construction firm. Although Gacy limited his homosexual encounters to times when his wife was out of town, the strain on his marriage was too much and the couple separated in 1976.

For Gacy, sex was rarely consensual. He pulled a gun on a youth who had come to him for work, threatening to shoot him if he did not have sex. The boy called his bluff, even though Gacy said that he had killed people before. This may well have been true. According to Gacy's own account, in January 1972 he had picked up a boy at a bus terminal and killed him. Nevertheless, his young employee in this instance escaped unmolested.

Gacy then developed a simple formula to ensnare victims. He would flash what appeared to be a police badge, pull a gun and tell his victim

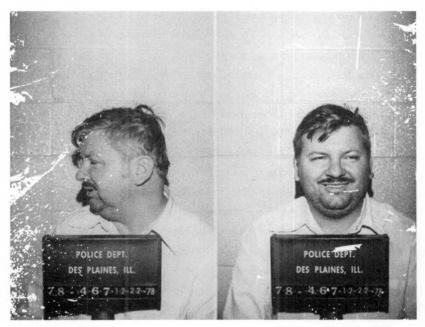

Gacy had a troubled childhood. His father was an abusive alcoholic who beat his wife and assaulted his children.

he was arresting him. Otherwise, he would invite teenage boys home, ply them with alcohol and then introduce them to his 'magic handcuffs'. Once manacled, he would sexually abuse his victims over a number of days. When he tired of his captives, he murdered them and buried them in the crawlspace underneath his house.

In 1977, Gacy was accused of sexually abusing a youth at gunpoint. Gacy admitted to having participated in brutal sex, but claimed that the boy had been a willing partner and was now trying to blackmail him. He was released with a caution.

By this time, Gacy was a successful contractor and a leading light in the local Democratic Party and was even photographed with the First Lady, Rosalynn Carter. And he entertained at children's parties, appearing as Pogo the Clown. He also hung out at notorious gay bars, picking up male prostitutes and ex-jailbirds as well as teenage runaways.

Gacy got tired of digging holes in his crawlspace, though there was a pressing need for more room to bury his victims. He hired one of his employees named David Cram to do the digging for him. Cram also stayed in the spare bedroom in his boss's house. One night, Cram came home from work and found Gacy drunk and in his clown costume. They had a few drinks and then Gacy tricked Cram into putting on his handcuffs. Gacy then turned nasty. He began spinning Cram around the room screaming: 'I'm going to rape you.' But Cram managed to push Gacy over, grabbed the key to the handcuffs and escaped.

Others also survived. In December 1977, Gacy abducted Robert Donnelly at gunpoint, tortured and sodomized him at his home, then let him go. Three months later, he picked up 27-year-old Jeffrey Rignall at one of his hangouts. He invited the young man to share a drink in his car. Once inside the sleek black Oldsmobile, Gacy held a rag soaked with chloroform over Rignall's face. When Rignall woke up, he was naked and strapped to a homemade rack in Gacy's basement. Gacy was also naked and showed Rignall a number of whips and more sinister sexual devices, explaining how he intended to use them. Gacy also told Rignall that he was a policeman and would shoot him if he raised any objection.

He beat his defenceless victim mercilessly. The abuse and torture went on for hours. At times, it was so painful that Rignall begged to be allowed to die. Gacy would chloroform him again, then wait until he came around before he began the torture all over again. Eventually, Rignall said that if Gacy let him go he would leave town and tell no one what had happened. He blacked out again, and woke up fully dressed by a lake in Chicago's Lincoln Park. There was money in his pocket but his driver's licence was missing.

In hospital, it was discovered that he was bleeding from the anus. His face was burnt and his liver was damaged by the chloroform. The police were sympathetic, but had little to go on. Rignall could not give them the name, address or licence plate of his assailant. But Rignall was determined. He rented a car and drove the route he thought Gacy had taken him, which he vaguely remembered through a haze of chloroform. Eventually, he found the expressway turn-off Gacy had taken. Waiting there, he struck lucky when Gacy's black Oldsmobile swept by. He noted down the licence plate number and followed the car to where it parked in the driveway of 8213 West Summerdale Avenue. Rignall even checked the land registry and found that the house belonged to John Wayne Gacy. Then he took the information to the police.

When they followed up on Rignall's leads, the Chicago Police Department found that Gacy's suburban home was just outside their jurisdiction, meaning they could not press felony charges against him. However, Gacy agreed to give Rignall $3,000 towards his medical bills and the matter was dropped. Despite this brush with the law, Gacy did not give up his campaign of abduction, sexual abuse and murder.

ATTRACTING THE AUTHORITIES' ATTENTION

In December 1978, Mrs Elizabeth Piest reported to the local police that her 15-year-old son Robert was missing. She had gone to collect him from the pharmacy where he had a part-time job, but Robert asked her to wait as he was going to visit a contractor who had promised him a summer job. He did not return and his parents spent the rest of the night driving around the streets looking for him, before reporting his disappearance.

The pharmacist told the police that the contractor concerned might have been John Gacy, who had recently refurbished his shop. The local police then phoned Gacy, but he denied all knowledge of the missing boy. Robert Piest was, in fact, lying dead on Gacy's bed as they spoke. Checking the records, the police discovered Gacy's earlier conviction for sodomy. They went to see him, but Gacy refused to come down to the precinct to discuss the matter and the police realized that they had no charge on which to hold him.

Instead, they put Gacy's house under 24-hour surveillance. Nevertheless, Gacy managed to put Piest's body in a trunk and smuggled it out to his car. He jumped behind the wheel and raced off at high speed, leaving the police standing. Having lost his tail, Gacy drove down to the nearby Des Plaines River, where he dumped Piest's body.

The police finally managed to get a search warrant, which was difficult as there was so little evidence to go on. In the house they found a receipt from the chemist for a roll of film made out to Kim Beyers, Robert's girlfriend. Although this wasn't enough to arrest Gacy, it was enough to justify putting him under further 24-hour surveillance. Meanwhile, checking back through the records in both Illinois and Iowa, they found details of his previous sexual offences.

Gacy must have thought he was untouchable and figured he could bluff this way through. He filed a civil lawsuit of $750,000 against the city of Des Plaines, alleging illegal search and seizure, harassment and slander. Then, one morning, he invited in two of the cops stationed outside his house for breakfast. As they sat down to eat, the policemen noticed a peculiar smell. Gacy had inadvertently switched off the pump that drained the basement. Water flowing under the house disturbed the soil where Gacy had buried 29 of his victims over the years and now the stench came up.

Armed with another warrant, the police discovered a trapdoor in the floor of a cupboard. When they opened it, they reeled back from the smell of rotting flesh that rose from the crawlspace below. A brief examination revealed a mass of human remains in a sea of stinking black mud. Gacy was immediately arrested and charged with murder.

INFAMY AND CELEBRITY
Sixteen bodies were found in the crawlspace, while another 11 had been buried in the ground around the house. Four more bodies – including Robert Piest's – were found in the Des Plaines River. Eight of them have never been identified. The youngest of his victims was nine; the oldest were full-grown men. John Wayne Gacy admitted killing 33 young men and boys over the previous seven years after having forced them to have sex with him. He was tried for mass murder in 1980.

One of those who testified against him was Jeffrey Rignall. His testimony did not last very long because he broke down while telling the court the details of his rape and torture. Rignall was so upset that he began to vomit and cry hysterically and was eventually removed from the courtroom. Gacy exhibited no sign of emotion throughout Rignall's harrowing account.

The defence sought to show that Gacy was insane. The jury disagreed and convicted Gacy of the murder of 33 young men. He was given 12 death sentences and 21 whole life sentences.

Despite his known homosexuality, on death row Gacy received fan mail from women. He studied law books and filed numerous appeals.

Though he had confessed, Gacy later denied his guilt and set up a premium-rate telephone number that featured a 12-minute recorded statement declaring his innocence.

While imprisoned at the Menard Correctional Center, Gacy took up studying the visual arts. His paintings were shown to the public in an exhibition at a Chicago gallery. Many of his pictures depict him in costume as Pogo the Clown. Others depict fellow serial killers Ed Gein and Jeffery Dahmer. Gacy was allowed to profit from their sale, with one painting fetching nearly $10,000. Some people bought his pictures with the sole intention of destroying them.

In October 1993, Gacy's final appeal was thrown out by the US Supreme Court and his death sentence was set for 10 May 1994. Gacy's last meal included a bucket of Kentucky Fried Chicken. Prison officers said he was 'chatty... talking up a storm'. In the press interview shortly before his execution, Gacy told a reporter: 'There's been 11 hardback books on me, 31 paperbacks, two screenplays, one movie, one off-Broadway play, five songs, and over 5,000 articles. What can I say about it?' Even though he was contributing to one more article, he quickly added: 'I have no ego for any of this garbage.'

Gacy was executed by lethal injection just after midnight on 10 May. His last words were 'Kiss my ass.' The following month, 25 of his paintings were burnt on a bonfire at an event in Naperville, just outside Chicago, attended by family members of nine of his victims.

Gacy's house at 8213 West Summerdale Avenue in Norwood Park, just east of Chicago's O'Hare International Airport, was torn apart in 1978 in an effort to find more evidence. The following year the site was cleared. One demolition worker said: 'If the devil's alive, he lived here.'

The empty lot attracted ghost hunters and other ghouls. A new house was built on the site, but it still attracted tourists and the occasional TV crew. A neighbour said: 'If you've got two guys in a car, or an out-of-state plate, it's probably Gacy.'

GARY RIDGWAY

The Green River Killer

GARY RIDGWAY ADMITTED KILLING 49 women between 1982 and 1984, dumping most of their bodies in or around the Green River in Washington state. There may have been many more. 'I killed so many women I have a hard time keeping them straight,' he said. The Green River Task Force worked on the case for nearly 20 years – even accepting advice at one point from notorious serial killer Ted Bundy, then on death row – until Ridgway was finally arrested in 2001.

On 15 July 1982, the body of 16-year-old Wendy Lee Coffield was found in the Green River east of Seattle. On 12 August the corpse of Debra Bonner, 23, was pulled from the same river, about half-a-mile upstream from where Wendy's body had been dumped. Detective Dave Reichert was assigned to the case. Three days later three more bodies – those of Marcia Faye Chapman, 31, Opal Charmaine Mills, 16, and Cynthia Jean Hinds, 17 – were found. They had all been strangled and a task force was set up to investigate what appeared to be a series of linked crimes.

Two earlier killings were not initially recognized as part of the series. On 21 January 1982, the body of 16-year-old Leann Wilcox was found in a field near Tacoma several miles from the river. A friend of Wendy Coffield, she too had been strangled. Then on 7 July 1982, 36-year-old Amina Agisheff disappeared. Her skeletal remains were not found and identified until April 1984.

The list of missing young women soon began to swell. Sixteen-year-old Kasee Ann Lee disappeared on 28 August. Ridgway admitted strangling her, but her body has never been found. Terry Rene Milligan went missing the following day. Three more teenagers disappeared in September. The killer claimed three more victims in October, and another two in December.

He killed twice the following March, five times in April and four more times in May. Between June 1983 and March 1984, Ridgway killed at least another 15. Then the murders became more sporadic. There were murders in 1987, 1990 and 1998 that Ridgway confessed to, along with another four where he was not sure of the date. He was suspected of another ten murders which he did not confess to, or there was not enough evidence for charges to be filed.

The killings tailed off after Ridgway began dating Judith Mawson, who became his third wife in 1988. Interviewed in prison, Ridgway said that his urge to kill declined once he was in a relationship with Mawson. It did not go away completely, though. When she moved into his house while they were dating, Mawson noticed there was no carpet. The police later told her Ridgway had probably used the carpet to wrap up a body.

Mawson said Ridgway would leave for work early in the morning some days and, later, assumed that he must have committed some of the murders while supposedly working those early shifts. She claimed that she had not suspected Ridgway before he was first contacted by the authorities in 1987 and had not even heard of the Green River Killer because she did not watch the news.

CUTTING A DEAL

For the Green River Task Force, Gary Ridgway's name had been in the frame since the beginning. In 1980, he was interviewed after a prostitute accused him of trying to throttle her. He said that she had bitten him and choked her to make her stop. The police picked him up with prostitute Kelly Kay McGinniss in 1982. She disappeared a year later and her body was never found.

Following the disappearance of 18-year-old Marie Malvar on 30 April 1983, Ridgway was a leading suspect. The police questioned him and he denied all knowledge of her, even though a friend of hers had seen Marie get into a truck that was thought to be Ridgway's. Her body was not found until September 2003, after Ridgway had finally confessed to her murder.

In May 1984 he took a lie detector test, but the polygraph cleared him. Nevertheless, Ridgway remained 'a person of interest'. In 1988, the police obtained a warrant to search his house, but found nothing incriminating. They also got permission to take a saliva sample to determine his blood group. Although DNA fingerprinting had been introduced in 1985, it was not then a reliable procedure if the amount of DNA was small. However, scientists later developed methods of amplification. In November 2001, samples saved from the earlier blood tests were subjected to DNA analysis and it was found that Ridgway's DNA matched that of semen recovered from the bodies of four victims of the Green River Killer.

Ridgway was arrested and charged with the murder of Marcia Chapman, Opal Mills, Cynthia Hinds and 21-year-old Carol Ann Christensen, who went missing on 4 May 1983 and was found four days later by a family picking mushrooms. Her body had been displayed in a particularly gruesome way. Her head was covered by a paper bag, with a fish placed on top of her neck. There was another fish on her left breast and a bottle between her legs. Her hands were crossed over her stomach with freshly ground beef placed on top of them. Her body showed signs of having been in water, even though the river was miles away. Ridgway pleaded not guilty to all charges when arraigned.

In March 2003, three more counts of murder were added, those of Debra Bonner, Wendy Coffield and 15-year-old Debra Estes, who went missing on 20 September 1982 and was not found until 30 May 1988 – after a forensic scientist identified microscopic spheres of paint of the type used at the Kenworth truck factory where Ridgway worked as a spray painter. Again, he pleaded not guilty.

However, just before his trial in November 2003 Ridgway entered into a plea bargain to avoid the death penalty. He confessed to 48 killings – although he said the total might be more than 60. As it was, the number he confessed to was more than the 41 on the Green River Task Force's list, but less that the 71 he was actually suspected of killing.

On 5 November 2003, Ridgway pleaded guilty to 48 counts of aggravated first-degree murder, saying that he had been motivated by a deep hatred for prostitutes.

'I wanted to kill as many women as I thought were prostitutes as I possibly could,' he said. 'I thought I could kill as many of them as I wanted without getting caught.'

However, not all of his victims had been prostitutes. Some were teenage runaways and drug addicts. Others seem to have been selected at random. He picked up women sometimes by showing them a picture of his son from his second marriage to engender trust.

After having sex with his victim, Ridgway strangled the woman from behind. Initially he did this manually. But when victims, trying to defend themselves, inflicted possibly incriminating wounds and bruises on his arm, he began to use ligatures to strangle his victims.

Most victims were killed in his home, in his truck, or in a secluded area. The bodies were often posed naked. They were left in clusters around certain areas, which gave Ridgway a thrill when he drove by. Sometimes he would return to a body and have sex with it. Later, he began burying his victims to remove that temptation.

A TROUBLED AND CONFUSED MAN

Ridgway was found to have a low IQ of just 82. As a boy he was a bed-wetter. His mother would use this to belittle him in front of his family. He admitted, from a young age, of having conflicted feelings of anger and sexual attraction towards her. At 16, he stabbed a six-year-old boy, saying he wondered what it would feel like to kill someone.

At 18, he joined the navy. Away from home a lot, Ridgway began to use prostitutes and his first wife also began to stray. His second wife accused him of trying to choke her. He became a religious zealot, while still using prostitutes. He also had an insatiable appetite for sex, forcing his wife to make love with him in public places, including areas where his victims' bodies were later discovered.

Before his sentencing, the families of Ridgway's victims were allowed to address the court.

'Gary Ridgway is an evil creature who I would condemn to many, many long years of anguish and despair,' said Nancy Gabbert, whose 17-year-old daughter, Sandra, was killed in 1983.

'I was only five when my mother died,' Sara King, daughter of Carol Ann Christensen, whose body was found in 1983, told him. 'The one thing I want you to know is that there was a daughter at home. I was that daughter... waiting for my mother to come home.'

The grieving relatives called Ridgway a coward, a monster, an animal, a devil, a vile killer and a paedophile. A handful angrily wished that he would burn in hell. More than a few said they hoped he would meet a violent end in prison.

'I can only hope that someday, someone gets the opportunity to choke you unconscious 48 times so you can live through the horror that you put our mothers and daughters through,' said Tim Meehan, brother of Mary Meehan, whose body was also found in 1983. 'To me you are already dead.'

Gary Ridgway was found to have an IQ of just 82. As a boy he was a bed-wetter and his mother used to belittle him in front of his family.

Ridgway turned slightly from the defence table to face the speakers, but he appeared largely unaffected by their words until Robert Rule approached the microphone. Ridgway had murdered his 16-year-old daughter, Linda, in 1982.

'Mr Ridgway, there are people here that hate you,' Robert Rule said. 'I'm not one of them. I forgive you for what you have done.'

As Rule spoke, Ridgway wiped away tears.

A statement from Ridgway's family was also read in court: 'Be assured that we were shocked to hear that Gary could do the things he has admitted to doing. However, we love Gary, and believe that the Gary Ridgway America now knows is different from the person known by our family. Clearly, there were two Gary Ridgways.'

Ridgway himself read an apology from a yellow legal pad.

'I know how horrible my acts were,' he said. 'I have tried for a long time to get these things out of my mind. I have tried for a long time to keep from killing any more ladies.'

He read in a halting tone, stopping to remove his glasses and wipe his eyes once more.

'I have tried hard to remember as much as I could to help the detectives find and recover the ladies,' he said, adding, 'I'm sorry for killing these ladies. They had their whole lives ahead of them.... I'm very sorry for the ladies that were not found. May they rest in peace. They need a better place than what I gave them.'

However, the judge dismissed Ridgway's emotions as 'Teflon-coated'.

'There is nothing in your life that was significant other than your own demented, calculating and lustful passion of being the emissary of death,' he said.

Ridgway was given 48 life sentences without the possibility of parole, plus another ten years for each victim for tampering with the evidence – giving him another 480 years to serve.

'You violated the sanctity of every relationship in your life,' the judge said. 'As you spend the balance of your life in your tiny cell surrounded only by your thoughts, please know that the women you killed were not throwaways or pieces of candy in a dish placed upon this planet for the sole purpose of satisfying your murderous desires.'

He asked Ridgway to turn around and look at the faces of the victims' relatives and friends who packed the courtroom.

'Mr Ridgway,' Judge Richard Jones said. 'Those are the families and friends of the people you killed. I truly hope that the last thoughts you have of the free world are of the faces of the people in this courtroom.'

Referring to Ridgway's method of strangling his victims from behind, the judge said: 'While you could not face them as you took their lives, if you have a drop of emotion anywhere in your existence, you will face those young women in your dreams.'

THE FINAL TALLY

In 2011, Ridgway pleaded guilty to a 49th murder – that of Rebecca 'Becky' Marrero, a 20-year-old mother last seen on 3 December 1982. Her skull was found in December 2010, not far from where Marie Malvar had been unearthed. Ridgway had already confessed to murdering her, but there was no evidence to charge him. Once the body part was identified by dental records, he submitted a guilty plea under the plea bargain he had entered into in 2003.

Ted Bundy had offered his help in the hunt for the person he called 'Riverman', fearing that the Green River killer would eclipse his reputation as a serial killer. During one interview session, Bundy suggested that the killer was most likely revisiting his dump sites to engage in sexual intercourse with the bodies. He advised the investigators in case they find a fresh grave to stake it out and wait for the killer to return. Bundy went to the electric chair before Ridgway was caught.

Another 'competitor' to Ridgway was Canadian serial killer Robert 'Willie' Pickton, who murdered prostitutes and other vulnerable women on his pig farm outside Vancouver. Although he boasted that he had killed more than Ridgway, he was finally convicted of the second-degree murder of six women in 2007, some way short of Ridgway's 49.

RICHARD RAMIREZ

The Night Stalker

As the Night Stalker, Richard Ramirez terrorized Los Angeles for two years. He was a devil worshipper whose calling card was a hastily scrawled pentagram and he made his rape victims declare their love of Satan before he slaughtered them. At his first court hearing after being apprehended, he raised a hand with his trademark pentagram drawn on it and yelled: 'Hail, Satan.'

The Night Stalker's murderous career began on the night of 8 June 1984, when the mutilated body of 79-year-old Jennie Vincow was found spread-eagled on the bed of her one-bedroom apartment in the Glassell Park district of Los Angeles. She had been raped and her throat had been slashed so violently that she had almost been decapitated. Fingerprints were found, but in those days comparisons had to be done manually so matching them with any that might be on file was a monumental task.

Nine months later, on 17 March 1985, Maria Hernandez had just parked her car in her garage in the Rosemead condominium when she was confronted by a man with a gun. He shot her. The bullet ricocheted off her car keys, but the impact of the bullet was enough to knock her to the ground. The gunman kicked her viciously, then made his way into her apartment. From inside, Maria heard a gunshot. She staggered to her feet, only to be confronted once more by the gunman running from the house.

'Please don't shoot me again,' she begged. The gunman froze, then took to his heels.

Inside the apartment Hernandez found her boyfriend, 34-year-old Hawaiian-born traffic manager Dayle Okazaki, lying on the kitchen floor, dead. He had been shot through the head.

THE 'NIGHT STALKER' IS BORN

There was only one clue to the murder. Maria said that the gunman had worn a baseball cap bearing the AC/DC logo. The Australian band had recently released an album called *Highway to Hell* which included a track called 'Night Prowler'. Although this was the *nom d'assassin* Ramirez would have preferred to have been known by, the newspapers instead dubbed him the Night Stalker.

The killer was not finished for the night. Less than an hour after killing Dayle Okazaki, he pulled 30-year-old Taiwanese law student Tsai Lian Yu from her car and shot her twice. She died before the ambulance arrived.

Ten days later, the killer entered the home of Vincent and Maxine Zazzara. Both of them were shot at point-blank range and Maxine's naked body was mutilated after death. She had been stabbed repeatedly and her eyes had been gouged out.

On 14 May 1985, Ramirez broke into a home in Monterey Park. He shot 66-year-old William Doi in the head while he lay sleeping. His disabled wife, 63-year-old Lillian, who was in bed next to him, was beaten around the head until she told the intruder where their valuables were hidden, after which he raped her.

A fortnight later, Carol Kyle was awoken in her Burbank apartment by a torch shining in her eyes. An armed man dragged her out of bed and raped and sodomized her. In the next room, Carol's terrified 12-year-old son had been locked in a closet. Her attacker ransacked the apartment and fled, leaving both Carol and her son alive.

Around the same time, two elderly women, 83-year-old Mabel Bell and her 80-year-old sister Florence Long, an invalid, were attacked in their home in the suburb of Monrovia. On 1 June, Florence was found lying on her bed in a coma. There was a huge wound over her ear and a bloodstained hammer was lying on the dressing table. Mabel was barely conscious on her bedroom floor in a pool of her own blood. An inverted pentagram, the encircled five-point star that is used in witchcraft, was scrawled in lipstick on Mabel's thigh. Another was drawn on Florence's bedroom wall. The police concluded that the two sisters had been left that way for two days. Six weeks after the attack, Mabel Bell died. Florence eventually regained consciousness and survived.

Then the Night Stalker's onslaught gained pace. On the night of 27 June, the killer slashed the throat of 32-year-old Patty Elaine Higgins in her home in Arcadia. The same fate befell 77-year-old Mary Louise Cannon five days later. Three days after that, again in Arcadia, Ramirez savagely beat 16-year-old Whitney Bennett with a tyre iron and throttled her with telephone wire. Somehow, she survived.

On 7 July, 61-year-old Joyce Lucille Nelson was found beaten to death in her home in Monterey Park and 63-year-old Sophie Dickman was raped and robbed in her apartment.

On 20 July, 68-year-old Max Kneiding and his 64-year-old wife Lela were shot and mutilated in their Glendale home. That same night 32-year-old Chainarong Khovananth was shot dead at his home in Sun Valley and his 29-year-old wife Somkid was raped and forced to perform oral sex. She was then beaten savagely and forced to swear in Satan's name that she would not cry out while he sodomized her eight-year-old son.

A PATTERN OF BEHAVIOUR EMERGES

The police were mystified. While these crimes were related, the killer had no clear modus operandi. He killed with guns, hammers and knives.

He raped orally, anally and genitally both children and women, young and old. Sometimes he mutilated the bodies after death, sometimes he let his victims live. Sometimes he stole; sometimes he didn't. However, there were some similarities between the crimes. The killer stalked quiet suburbs where homeowners were less security conscious. Entry was through an open window or an unlocked door. He made his attacks close to freeways, making escape easier. Pentagrams and other satanic symbols were commonly left by the killer, and his crimes were distinguished by their sheer brutality.

On the night of 5 August, Virginia Petersen was shot in the face in her Northridge home. The bullet entered the cheek just below her eye and went clean through the back of her head. Her husband Christopher then got a bullet in the temple. But he was a tough guy and flung himself at the intruder, who panicked and ran. Both miraculously survived to give a detailed description of their attacker.

Three days later, 35-year-old Elyas Abowath was shot dead at his home in Diamond Bar and his 28-year-old wife was beaten and raped. Again, she was forced to swear by Satan that she would not cry out.

The residents of Los Angeles were now on the alert. Locksmiths were doing a roaring trade and gun shops quickly sold out. But the killer simply travelled north to San Francisco. On the night of 17 August 1985, 66-year-old accountant Peter Pan was shot dead in his home in the suburb of Lake Merced. His 64-year-old wife Barbara was also shot as she fought off the attacker, but survived. An inverted pentagram was drawn in lipstick on the bedroom wall along with the words 'Jack the Knife'. At first, the police thought it was a copy-cat attack, but the bullets matched the small-calibre rounds found in the Los Angeles murders.

A week later, in the small town of Mission Viejo, 80 km (50 miles) south of Los Angeles, 29-year-old computer engineer William Carns was shot three times in the head and his fiancée Inez Erickson, also 29, was raped. The attacker announced that he was the Night Stalker and forced her to say 'I love Satan' during her ordeal.

Inez saw a rusty old orange Toyota drive off after the attacker left the house. This proved to be the vital clue that put an end to the reign of the Night Stalker. A sharp-eyed kid, James Romero III, had also spotted the orange Toyota and noted its licence plate. Two days later, the car was found in a parking lot in the Los Angeles suburb of Rampart.

A single fingerprint was found, and it was matched to those of 25-year-old Ricardo 'Richard' Ramirez, a petty criminal who had been arrested three times for marijuana possession. Soon his photograph was on the front page of every newspaper in California.

THE PEOPLE VERSUS RICHARD RAMIREZ

Ramirez had been out in Phoenix, Arizona, to score some cocaine and was quite unaware of his new-found fame as he stepped down from the Greyhound bus at Los Angeles' main bus station at about 8.30 am on 31 August 1985. He was high. By then he had killed 13 people and he felt good. Surely, he must be Satan's favourite son.

He went into a local shop to buy a Pepsi. At the checkout he saw his own face splashed across the Spanish language paper *La Opinion*. The checkout clerk recognized him. So did the other customers. The game was up and Ramirez made a run for it.

Out on the street, someone cried out: 'It's the Night Stalker!'

Ramirez ran out on to the Santa Ana Freeway and tried to carjack a woman but was forced to flee by a crowd pursuing him. He ran for just over 3 km (2 miles). As he paused to catch his breath he was surrounded by the wail of police sirens. Desperate to get off the street, he knocked on a door at random. Bonnie Navarro opened it. Ramirez shouted 'Help me' in Spanish. She slammed the door in his face.

On the next block, he tried to pull a woman from her car, but bystanders again rushed to her rescue. Ramirez then jumped over a

Richard Ramirez – a sharp-eyed kid spotted his rusty old orange Toyota. Two days later, the car was found in the Los Angeles suburb of Rampart.

fence into a backyard where Luis Muñoz was cooking a barbecue. He hit Ramirez with his tongs. In the next yard, Ramirez tried to steal a red 1966 Mustang, but 56-year-old Faustino Pinon, who was working on the transmission, grabbed him in a headlock. Ramirez broke free and ran on, pursued by Pinon.

Angelina de la Torres was about to get into her gold Granada when she saw Ramirez running towards her screaming: 'I'm going to kill you.' She hit him with the car door. Her husband Manuel heard the fracas. He came out of the house with a metal pole in his hand and ran towards Ramirez. From the other side of the street 55-year-old construction worker Jose Burgoin and his two sons, Jaime and Julio, all ran after Ramirez. Now he had five men chasing him.

Manuel de la Torres caught up with Ramirez and struck him three times with the metal pole. Ramirez fell to the ground and Jose, Jaime and Julio jumped on top of him. Just then, a patrol car screeched to a halt in front of the group of men.

'Save me!' yelled Ramirez. As a patrolman handcuffed him, he said: 'Thank God you came. I am the one you want. Save me before they kill me.'

Safely in custody, Ramirez showed no contrition for his crimes. In fact, he relished them. He told the police: 'I love to kill people. I love watching them die. I would shoot them in the head and they would wiggle and squirm all over the place, and then just stop. Or I would cut them with a knife and watch their faces turn real white. I love all that blood. I told one lady one time to give me all her money. She said no. So I cut her and pulled her eyes out.'

On 20 September 1989, Richard Ramirez was found guilty on 13 counts of murder, five attempted murders, 11 sexual assaults and 14 burglaries. He was given 12 death sentences, along with a sentence of over 100 years' imprisonment. Sentencing him, the judge said that

Ramirez demonstrated 'cruelty, callousness and viciousness beyond any human understanding'.

Asked if he had anything to say, Ramirez replied: 'I have a lot to say, but now is not the time or place. I don't know why I am wasting my breath. But what the hell, I don't believe in the hypocritical moralistic dogmas of this so-called civilized society. You maggots make me sick. Hypocrites one and all! You don't understand me. You are not expected to. You are not capable of it. I am beyond your experience. I am beyond good and evil.'

Peter Zazzara, the son of the murdered Vincent and Maxine, said after the trial: 'I don't know why somebody would want to do something like that. To take joy in the way it happened.'

Ramirez wasn't bothered. On his way to San Quentin where the gas chamber awaited, he said: 'Hey, big deal. Death comes with the territory. I'll see you in Disneyland.'

While he was on death row, many women wrote to Ramirez, some sending provocative pictures, pledging undying love and proposing marriage. In 1996 he married Doreen Lioy in San Quentin. She had written him some 75 letters in prison. She told CNN: 'I think he's a really great person. He's my best friend; he's my buddy.' Although she threatened to take her own life if Richard was executed, the marriage did not last and they divorced after a few years. In total, the trial cost $1.8 million and was California's most expensive legal proceeding until that of O.J. Simpson. It generated 50,000 pages of trial papers. Marshalling those meant that the first appeal did not even begin until 7 August 2006. Ramirez's lawyer then argued that his client was possessed by the devil and a helpless victim of his own sexuality, so he should not be sentenced to death.

'Life imprisonment without parole means he will never see Disneyland again,' he said.

The California Supreme Court upheld both the convictions and the death sentence. However, Ramirez escaped the gas chamber, dying of liver failure in 2013 at the age of 53. During his 23 years on death row, he never admitted to his crimes nor showed any remorse for what he had done.

SAMUEL LITTLE

The Craziest Rap Sheet

AFTER SAMUEL LITTLE HAD been arrested for the murder of three women in Los Angeles a quarter of a century earlier, Deputy District Attorney Beth Silverman, who has worked on many serial killer cold cases, said Little had 'the craziest rap sheet I've ever seen'.

It was more than 100 pages long and listed crimes – including assault, burglary, armed robbery, shoplifting and drug violations – in 24 US states spread over 56 years. Arrested more than 50 times, Little had served less than ten years in prison.

'The fact that he hasn't spent a more significant period of his life in custody is a shocking thing,' said Silverman. 'He's gotten break after break after break.'

Convicted of the three murders in LA in 2014 and sentenced to life imprisonment without the possibility of parole, Little still protested his innocence. But following his arrest prosecutors across the US opened their cold-case files and by 2018 Little was confessing to more slayings, boasting in the end that he had killed more than 93 souls, a total that would have made him America's most prolific serial killer. However, the authorities could only link him to 61 deaths, just eight of which have been confirmed.

A CATALOGUE OF CRIMES

Born in 1940, Little was a poor student and was first convicted for burglary in Omaha, Nebraska, at the age of 16. This earned him time in

Samuel Little has confessed to 93 murders in 19 states over 35 years. The FBI has verified 50 of these cases so far, making him the most prolific serial killer in US history.

an institution for juvenile offenders. Just months after he was released, Little was arrested again for breaking and entering. He began boxing in jail and claims to have had a brief career as a prize-fighter.

Having been brought up by his grandmother in Lorain, Ohio, Little went to live with his mother in Florida in his late 20s. He worked at the Dade County Department of Sanitation and, later, at a cemetery. Then, often using the name Samuel McDowell, he began travelling more widely and had further run-ins with the law. Between 1971 and 1975, Little was arrested 26 times in 11 states for crimes that included assault, armed robbery, rape, theft, solicitation of a prostitute, breaking and entering, shoplifting, driving under the influence, aggravated assault on a police officer and fraud. Interviewed by LA detectives, he described these crimes as 'shoplifting and, uh, petty thefts and stuff'.

Then, in 1976, Pamela Kay Smith knocked on the back door of a home in Sunset Hills, Missouri. She was naked from the waist down and her hands were tied behind her with electrical cable. The homeowners called 911 and Smith told the police that Little had attacked her. He had picked her up in St Louis, some 24 km (15 miles) away. She said he had choked her with the cable, forced her into his car, beat her until she was unconscious, then drove her to Sunset Hills where he raped her.

Little was found sitting in his car near the house where Pamela had sought refuge. He had with him items of her clothing and her jewellery. He denied raping her, telling officers: 'I only beat her.' He was found guilty of assault with the intent to ravish-rape and was sentenced to just three months in county jail. This may have been because he pleaded guilty to a lesser charge as Pamela Kay Smith was a heroin addict who often failed to make scheduled court appearances.

In October 1982, the skeletal remains of 22-year-old Melinda 'Mindy' LaPree were found in a cemetery in Gautier, Mississippi. She had last been seen in nearby Pascagoula a month before, getting into a brown wood-panelled station wagon with a man witnesses later identified as Little. During the investigation, two prostitutes came forward and alleged that Little had also assaulted them in Pascagoula in 1980 and 1981.

In November, Little was arrested for shoplifting in Pascagoula. The police spotted that he matched the description of the suspect in the LaPree slaying. He was charged with murder and the aggravated assaults of the two other prostitutes, but a grand jury failed to indict.

He was extradited to Florida to face another murder charge. In September 1982, the body of Patricia Ann Mount had been found in the countryside outside Forest Grove, Gainesville. Twenty-six-year-old Mount, who was mentally disabled, was last seen leaving a beer tavern with a man identified as Little in a wood-panelled station wagon. However, the trial hinged on hairs found on Mount's clothes that 'had the same characteristics as head hairs taken from Little', according to a forensic scientist. But when cross-examined the analyst said: 'It was also possible for hairs to be transferred if two people bumped together.' Little was acquitted and released.

In October 1984, Little was back in custody in San Diego, accused of the attempted murder of two prostitutes who were kidnapped a month apart. They had been driven to the same abandoned dirt lot, assaulted and choked. The first woman was left unconscious on a pile of rubbish, but survived. Officers found Little in a car with the second woman and arrested him.

The two cases were tried together, but the jury failed to reach a verdict. Pleading guilty to lesser charges of assault with great bodily injury and false imprisonment, Little served about 30 months of a four-year sentence and was released on parole in February 1987.

He then moved to Los Angeles. Soon after, two women were found dead. They were 41-year-old Carol Alford, found in an alley in South LA, and 35-year-old Audrey Nelson, dumped in a dustbin downtown. Both had been strangled and were naked below the waist. In 1989, 46-year-old Guadalupe Apodaca was found dead in similar circumstances in an abandoned garage. DNA was collected from the bodies.

For the next 16 years, Little continued to have brushes with the law in seven states for driving under the influence, burglary, larceny, theft and shoplifting, among other offences. In the following five years, arresting officers noted that there were outstanding warrants against him in other states. But the charges were non-extraditable and he was released.

THE MURDERS MOUNT UP

In 2007, Little was arrested in Los Angeles for possession of cocaine. He pleaded guilty and was sentenced to a drug aversion programme, which he failed to attend. A judge issued a bench warrant, but Little had left the state so it could not be served.

It was not until 2012 that the LAPD matched the DNA in the Alford, Nelson and Apodaca murder cases to Little. Then, early in 2013, after being arrested for the possession of a crack pipe, he was found in a homeless shelter in Louisville, Kentucky. Charged with three counts of murder, Samuel Little was returned to California.

The scope of the trial was broadened when two prostitutes testified about their near misses with Little. Leila Johnson escaped strangling to flee topless into heavy shipyard traffic in November 1981. In her early 20s, she had fought off his brutal attack.

'He got his big hands around my neck, but I'm a fighter and I was scratching him in the eyeballs, kicking and fighting, fighting, fighting,' she said. 'He was evil. You could tell he hated women and he liked having control.'

When Johnson escaped Little's station wagon in 1981, she had run through woods and on to US Route 90 – dodging vehicles – and finally fell at the feet of a man who helped her. She did not report her attack at the time.

'I didn't think anybody would care or believe me,' she said. Her verdict on Little was: 'He preyed on the weak. He preyed on people he could use and abuse and kill.'

Another Pascagoula prostitute who sought anonymity was badly injured. In July 1980, she said he entered her home, knocked her unconscious and pulled a scarf tightly around her neck.

'He put me in a bathtub and was submerging my head in and out of the water,' said the victim, who was unconscious for most of the attack. 'I think he was trying to bring me to before he took me to my bedroom to choke me to death. It probably wouldn't have been any fun for him to choke me while I was expressionless.... He beat me severely, and I guess the only reason he didn't kill me is because a friend of mine came and knocked on my door.' She woke up in hospital. Her case was not investigated, however, until a white girl turned up dead two years later, she said.

That was Mindy LaPree, whose murder case was re-opened in Mississippi. Little was then investigated for his involvement with the murder of 60 other women in various states.

According to Pascagoula detective Darren Versiga who worked on the LaPree cold case and also testified in the California trial, Little was a 'professional shoplifter'.

'He was a thief by day and a murderer by night,' Versiga said. 'He would steal, steal, steal all day long and then flash his money to get these girls in his car and then strangle them.'

Four years after his first murder convictions, Little began making confessions in exchange for a transfer out of the Los Angeles County prison where he was being held. Often, he was taken to other states to assist in their investigations.

Little confessed to strangling Melissa Thomas in Opelousas, Louisiana, in 1996. He pleaded guilty to the murder of Denise Christie Brothers in Odessa, Texas, in 1994 and was given another life sentence. He admitted the murder of 23-year-old Brenda Alexander, whose naked body was found on a dirt road in Phenix City, Alabama, in 1979. Little described leaving a Columbus dance club with her in the early morning hours of 26 August.

'He wringed his hands together, smiled and said, "I knew she was mine,"' said an investigator.

In Macon, Georgia, he said he had strangled 18-year-old Fredonia Smith and an unidentified woman in 1977. Little also confessed to the 1982 murder of 55-year-old Dorothy Richards and the 1996 murder of 40-year-old Daisy McGuire. Both bodies were found in Houma, Louisiana.

Thirty-six-year-old Julia Critchfield was strangled in Harrison County, Mississippi, in 1978 and her body dumped off a cliff. The mother of four children was last seen at Chris's Lounge on Courthouse Road in Gulfport. Little admitted to killing 46-year-old Nancy Carol Stevens in Tupelo, Mississippi, 19-year-old Evelyn Weston, whose body was found near Fort Jackson, South Carolina in 1978, and 20-year-old Rosie Hill in Marion County, Florida, in 1982.

In 2018, the FBI's Violent Criminal Apprehension Program team had confirmed 34 of Little's confessions and was working to match the remainder to known murders or suspicious deaths, though Little often did not know the name or age of his victims. However, he often provided sketches to help investigators.

METHOD IN HIS MADNESS

Little's method of killing didn't always leave obvious signs that the death was a homicide. As a one-time boxer, Little usually stunned or knocked out his victims with powerful punches and then strangled them. With no stab marks or bullet wounds, many of these deaths were attributed to drug overdoses, accidents or natural causes.

In December 2018, Little was indicted for the murder of 23-year-old Linda Sue Boards in Warren County, Kentucky, in May 1981. In May 2019, he was indicted on four counts of aggravated murder and six counts of kidnapping in Cuyahoga County, Ohio. Little was convicted ot two more murders in August 2019: Rose Evans in Cleveland, Ohio in August 1991 and a 'Jane Doe' in Cincinnati between 1980 and 1999.

At the age of 79, Little was in poor health and seemed likely to stay in prison in Texas until his death. There he struck up a rapport with Texas Ranger James Holland.

'People for years have been trying to get a confession out of him and James Holland is the one who finally got him to give that information,' said the district attorney in Ector County, Texas, Bobby Bland. 'If all of these are confirmed, he'll be the most prolific serial killer, with confirmed killings, in American history. So far we don't have any false information coming from him.'

Little told investigators he targeted women who would not be missed, such as homeless people or sex workers.

'To him, strangulation was sex,' said Mark Piepmeier, Hamilton County chief assistant prosecutor. 'That's how bizarre this person is.'

Cincinnati detective Kelly Best said: 'He described it as telling a normal man that normal sexual intercourse was a crime. And when he got the urge, that's when he would seek out a woman and commit his crimes.'

She and Piepmeier said Little seemed to be trying to help. 'He was friendly, conversational, very open, very helpful,' Best said, adding that there appeared to be nothing about him that would give 'a vibe' of danger. Others, though, described him as 'evil'.

Franklin county prosecutor Ron O'Brien said: 'You think you've seen it all... but then something new happens and you shake your head.'

The goal of the Violent Criminal Apprehension Program was to identify Little's victims and provide closure and justice in unsolved cases. A map on the FBI's website says Little told investigators he killed women in Arizona, Arkansas, California, Georgia, Florida, Illinois, Louisiana, Maryland, Mississippi, Nevada, Ohio, South Carolina, Tennessee and Texas, but not all of the killings have been confirmed.

PATRICK MACKAY

The Devil's Disciple

FEW PEOPLE WHO KNEW Patrick Mackay can have been surprised when he was arrested for murder in 1975. Seven years earlier Home Office psychiatrist Dr Leonard Carr had predicted that he would become 'a cold psychopathic killer'. Indeed, after quickly admitting the murder he had been arrested for, Mackay confessed to ten other killings over the previous two years.

Mackay's troubles began before he was born. His father Harold had kicked his mother Marion in the stomach when she was pregnant. Harold was a disturbed individual, having served in North Africa during the Second World War. He had been leading a patrol near Alexandria that had been ambushed. He was the only survivor and had been wounded. A metal plate inserted in his arm gave him trouble for the rest of his life.

In 1947, Harold's first wife died in childbirth. Three years later he took a job as a bookkeeper on a sugar plantation in what was then British Guiana, now Guyana. There he met and married Marion, a good-looking Creole woman. They returned to England where Patrick was born in 1952. Two sisters soon followed.

In London, Harold took a dead-end job as an accountant. It made him enough money to buy a semi-detached house in Dartford, Kent. But he was disappointed with his lot in life. Consoling himself with drink, he became an abusive alcoholic.

'My father used to get violently drunk, shout, scream and always when he was like this beat me with the back of his hand and sometimes his fist,' recalled Mackay. 'He must have had a tremendous drinking problem, but of course he would never say so. I remember that my father never at all hit my two sisters when drunk, but only me and my mother. He would make a lot of filthy accusations towards her. This would take place usually Friday nights and Saturday nights. It was plain bloody regular.'

At school, Patrick took revenge on smaller children, particularly girls – including his younger sister. He stole and lied, and was an all-round troublemaker. There was no respite at home. The police were called regularly to restrain his father, who spent so much money on drink that the house began to deteriorate. At one point there was no hot water. The children and their clothes grew filthy. When his father was not abusing Patrick, he was regaling him with his reminiscences of the desert war, particularly the ambush and the gruesome manner of his comrades' deaths.

Patrick was ten when his father suddenly died. He refused to accept it. For years afterwards he lied, telling people Harold was still alive. He carried a picture of his father in his army uniform everywhere and claimed that he heard his voice.

He became violent and abusive towards his mother and sisters, threw tantrums and had fits, falling to the ground frothing at the mouth. In the autumn of 1963, Patrick's mother had a nervous breakdown and was admitted to hospital. Patrick was taken into care before being sent to a foster mother. However, his mother was eventually discharged and the children were returned to her.

BECOMING A JUVENILE DELINQUENT

Patrick's violent rages were then taken out on animals. His pet dog was attacked remorselessly. He tortured his pet rabbit and tried to strangle a neighbour's cat. His tortoise was grilled alive on a bonfire and he played with dead birds that he may have killed himself. He also speculated aloud about his father's decaying bones.

He bullied younger children, threatened an old woman with a pitchfork and set fire to a neighbour's garden shed. The theft of some garden gnomes marked the beginning of his criminal record. In juvenile court for the first time at the age of 11, he had 21 charges taken into consideration and was given three years' probation.

Truanting from school, he would barricade himself in the house, or smash the place up. The police were called and he was referred to a psychiatrist. After further outbursts Patrick was sent to the adolescent unit of a nearby hospital, where it was noted that he took a doll to bed with him and kissed it goodnight. He ran away three times. Again, he found himself in the juvenile court for theft.

He was sent to an Approved School where he was caned regularly. One of the masters wrote: 'He is a potential murderer of women.'

After absconding several times, he found himself in a psychiatric unit. Having been discharged, in 1968 Patrick Mackay tried to strangle his mother. When the police arrived, they found him trying to commit suicide. He was sent to a mental hospital. Two days after his release he was charged with assaulting two boys. Mackay was sentenced to two years' probation. More assaults followed and a court sent him to Moss Side mental hospital in Manchester, certified as a diagnosed psychopath. He was discharged in 1970, returning home to continue abusing his mother and sisters.

Barely literate, he was found a job as a gardener's labourer with Kensington and Chelsea Borough Council. An aunt in west London took him in. He tried to strangle her. By then, he was a regular user of drink and drugs.

Returning to his mother, there was more domestic violence. When the police intervened, they found his bedroom was full of Nazi memorabilia. Sent back to mental hospital, Mackay absconded again. On his return, it was noted that he was violent and seemingly obsessed with death.

After another stretch in Moss Side, he was found another job, but was sacked after ten days, having only turned up twice. He stayed with friends, who he abused, and became more obsessed with the Nazis, even making himself a rudimentary uniform. His mother's mixed blood then became a concern. Failing to pick up his benefits, he supported himself instead by burglary.

DEMON DRINK AND SAINTLY PRIESTS

In May 1973, Patrick Mackay was befriended by Father Anthony Crean, who lived in the village of Shorne, just outside Gravesend, in Kent. Father Crean took him to the pub and bought him drinks. One night, Mackay broke into Crean's cottage and stole a cheque for £30. He changed the £30 to £80 and cashed it. When Mackay was arrested, Father Crean tried to get the charges against him dropped, but the police insisted that the prosecution go ahead.

Mackay pleaded guilty and was fined £20 for breaking and entering with a two-year conditional discharge and was ordered to repay the £80 to Father Crean at £7 a week. Mackay went to see Father Crean and promised to repay him, a promise he never kept.

Unable to hold down a job and all too often drunk and abusive, Mackay found himself with nowhere to live. On 14 July 1974, the police found Mackay drunk and unconscious in the street and took him to St Thomas's Hospital in London.

The following day, he was arrested for chasing a tramp with a long metal pole and throwing bricks down a pedestrian subway. He then became abusive, claiming that he was a 'pure Aryan' and he would kill all 'Jewish bastards'. He later claimed to have been drunk and had no recollection of the incident. However, the police insisted that he was not drunk and that his behaviour was 'manifestly manic'.

While he was found guilty, sentencing was deferred for six months. Four days later he was back in court for being drunk and disorderly, and damaging a public lavatory. He was fined £15 and ordered to pay £10.44 for the damage he had caused. Two weeks later he was stopped riding a stolen child's bike, drunk, without lights at night. Unable to raise the £5 bail – or find anyone to post it for him – he spent three weeks on remand in Pentonville Prison, north London before being fined £25.

A kindly Anglican priest took him in as a lodger in his house in Finchley. He got a job as a gardener, which he liked. Back in court for sentencing in February 1974, he was given two months, once again suspended.

Some of the police involved in Mackay's later murder case think that he had probably killed five people by this time. Mackay admitted only one. After being arrested for murder in 1975, he said that in January 1974 he had thrown a tramp off Hungerford Bridge into the Thames. On average, three bodies a month are found in the river. None could be linked to the incident Mackay described. Lacking evidence, no charges were brought.

He found work as a groundsman, then as a keeper on Hadley Woods Common. In the evenings, he would get drunk. After a drunken row with one of his few friends, he decided to kill himself, but a policeman stopped him and took him to Tooting Bec Hospital. There he admitted to having been under psychiatric care since the age of 17 and that he enjoyed the company of murderers and psychopaths.

It was concluded that Mackay was not mentally ill – that is, a schizophrenic or depressive. Rather, he had a psychopathic personality disorder. But that was no grounds for holding him. Instead, social services were informed and he was discharged.

Three days earlier, he had met 84-year-old widow Isabella Griffiths in Chelsea and helped carry her shopping. She invited him into her home at 19 Cheyne Walk, a tall house set back from the River Thames, and offered him a drink. When Mackay left, she gave him £5 and told him to drop in whenever he was in the area.

After being discharged from hospital, he went straight there. Mrs Griffiths opened the door, but kept it on a safety chain, saying that she did not want any shopping that day. He asked to come in. When she refused, Mackay pushed against the door hard enough to break the chain.

He throttled her and dragged her into the kitchen, then paused to listen to the news on the radio. According to his own account, he wandered around the house before he felt 'a strong compulsion to kill her outright'. In the kitchen, he found a large knife and stabbed Mrs Griffiths in the solar plexus. Sitting in the front room, he drank a bottle of whisky he had brought with him. Then he pulled the knife from his victim's body and thought momentarily of stabbing himself, but the suicidal feeling passed.

He closed Mrs Griffiths' eyes, crossed her arms and covered her body. Then he tidied up. After stealing a mahogany cigarette box, he locked up and left, throwing the knife into a garden.

The widow's body was not found for 12 days, when the police had to force entry into her home. The stab wound was not noticed until the corpse was in the mortuary. With little to go on, the murder remained unsolved for a year.

Back in Finchley, Mackay took to making model aircraft – black ones with swastikas on them. He also made toy monsters and burned their eyes out. Otherwise he would spend his evenings in a rambling discourse with his landlord, the priest, about the nature of evil and possession.

When Mackay and the priest eventually fell out, his aunt found digs for him. But in July 1974, he returned to Finchley and broke into

In 1975, Patrick Mackay appeared at the Old Bailey charged with murdering five people. He used to spend evenings with his landlord, a priest, discussing the nature of evil and possession.

the priest's home. Two days later Mackay was arrested and charged with burglary. Found guilty, he was sentenced to four months in Wormwood Scrubs. With nowhere to go when he was released, he was lodged in a hostel.

OFF THE STREETS AT LAST, AT A HEAVY PRICE

Mackay had long paid for his excessive drinking by snatching elderly ladies' handbags. On 10 March 1975, he followed 89-year-old Adele Price home to Lowndes Square where she had a third-floor flat. He tricked his way in and throttled her.

'I felt hellish and very peculiar inside,' he said. 'This peculiar feeling I had for some days before and after each killing.'

Mackay watched television and fell asleep. He was awoken by Mrs Price's granddaughter who could not get in because he had secured the safety chain on the front door. When she returned, it had been taken off and Mackay had made his escape. The police only realized that Mrs Price had been murdered because Mackay had left her body in the bedroom and locked the door from the outside.

Two days later, Mackay walked off the platform at Stockwell underground station, hoping to be hit by a train, but alert staff turned the electricity off. The police took him to a mental hospital, but after five days' observation he was again discharged.

Following a spate of handbag snatching over the next two days, he took the train to Kent carrying two sharp kitchen knives. Mackay walked into Father Crean's cottage, saying he had come to discuss the money he owed him. Crean made for the front door.

Mackay grabbed him. They tussled. Crean said: 'Don't hurt me.'

'This seemed to get me even more excitable myself,' recalled Mackay, who started punching his former good samaritan.

Crean fled into the bathroom. Mackay grabbed an axe from under the stairs. He forced his way in. Pushing Crean into the bath, he stabbed him in the neck, then struck him on the head with the axe with such force that the priest's brain was exposed. Crean raised his hand to touch the wound, then died.

The body was discovered by the mother superior of nearby St Catherine's Convent, where Father Crean was chaplain. When considering possible suspects, the local police recalled the case where Father Crean had tried to prevent the prosecution of Mackay.

They quickly traced him to his probation hostel, and from there to the home of a friend, where he was arrested. In custody, he admitted ten other murders and was charged with five. Two of those charges were dropped due to lack of evidence. Convicted, he was still in jail over 40 years later; as he was convicted under a 'whole life tariff' he is unlikely ever to be released.

KIMBERLY CLARK SAENZ

The Bleach Killer

IN APRIL 2008, INSPECTORS of the Texas Department of Health Services were alerted to problems at the DaVita Dialysis clinic in Lufkin, Texas. A member of the emergency services sent an anonymous letter saying: 'In the last two weeks, we have transported 16 patients. This seems a little abnormal and disturbing to my med crews. Could these calls be investigated by you?'

Reviewing the clinic's record, it was found that there had only been two emergency calls in the previous 15 months, but they had been called out 30 times that month – seven for cardiac problems. Four people had already died. On 1 April, Clara Strange and Thelma Metcalf died after suffering cardiac arrest. On the 16th, Garlin Kelley suffered cardiac arrest and died two days later at the hospital, while Graciela Castañeda lost consciousness during treatment.

On 22 April, Cora Bryant suffered cardiac arrest and died three months later at the hospital. The following day, Marie Bradley suffered a severe drop in blood pressure. Then on 26 April, Opal Few died after suffering cardiac arrest and Debra Oates experienced multiple symptoms and a severe drop in blood pressure.

Concerned about the mortality rate, DaVita sent in a new supervisor from Houston named Amy Clinton who promptly took charge. When

34-year-old Kimberly Saenz arrived on shift at 4.30 am on 28 April, she was distressed to find that she had effectively been demoted. She was in tears. Previously, she had the run of the place. Her job as a nurse was to move from patient to patient, injecting medication into the dialysis lines and ports with a syringe. Now she was to clean up after patients, wiping up blood and vomit.

At around 6 am, Marva Rhone and Carolyn Risinger came into the clinic. Like other patients with failed kidneys, they spent hours on the dialysis machine cleansing their blood three times a week. It was a matter of life and death.

Two other patients, Lurlene Hamilton and Linda Hall, sitting nearby, noticed that Saenz was nervous. They saw her squat down and pour bleach into her cleaning bucket. Then they saw her draw up the caustic liquid into a syringe. At the very least, they thought this insanitary. But then they said they saw her inject the contents of the syringe into the dialysis lines of Rhone and Risinger.

Hamilton told Amy Clinton what she and seen, adding: 'I'm a little nervous right now, and I'm worried because she's assigned to me.'

Linda Hall also reported that Saenz had filled a syringe and injected Rhone's 'saline' line. Both witnesses said they saw Saenz dispose of the syringes in the DaVita sharps containers. Shortly after, Rhone and Risinger experienced a dramatic drop in blood pressure.

After speaking to Hamilton and Hall, Clinton asked Saenz whether she had administered any medication that day. Saenz said no. When asked about the bleach, Saenz explained that she 'was drawing up bleach to mix for her containers' that she had on the floor. Three syringes collected from the sharp container tested positive for bleach. She then acknowledged using a syringe to extract the bleach from its container because she was concerned about being precise and following procedures. A solution of bleach was commonly used to sterilize equipment in the clinic, but she adamantly denied ever injecting bleach into a patient.

Kimberly Saenz was seen injecting bleach into the dialysis lines of patients in the hospital where she worked.

Saenz was sent home. The following day the clinic was closed as an investigation was carried out. A meeting was called to inform the employees. All of them turned up except for Saenz. Co-worker Werlan Guillory phoned her and asked: 'Where are you? Are you coming to the meeting?'

Saenz said she could not make it.

'I'm a chaperone at my daughter's field day,' she said.

Guillory expressed concern that Saenz might lose her job, but Saenz simply responded: 'Okay.'

After the meeting, Guillory went to find Saenz. He said she was uncharacteristically unkempt and acted as if she did not recognize him. She was crying and told him she 'didn't kill those people'. This was unexpected as, at that point, no one had made any allegations that someone was killing patients. Guillory described Saenz as seeming 'like she had lost all the hope in the world'.

A CHEQUERED PAST

Saenz had held her entry-level position as a Licensed Vocational Nurse (LVN) at the clinic for nine months by then. Previously, she had been fired from another hospital in Lufkin for stealing the opioid Demerol, which was found in her handbag. She had also been arrested for public intoxication and criminal trespass, and the police had been called for domestic disturbances involving her husband, Mark Kevin Saenz. He filed for divorce and had obtained a restraining order against Saenz in June 2007, just a few months before she began at DaVita. An examination of the records revealed that 84 per cent of the time patients had suffered from chest pain or cardiac arrest, Saenz had been on duty.

Questioned by Lufkin police officers, Saenz was noticeably upset that two patients had accused her of giving them another patient's medication. Asked why she had not attended the meeting, Saenz said she was scared to go to work because DaVita 'can't tell us what's going on, and I'm doing everything by the book, and I'm scared because I have a licence'. She added: 'If I'm doing something wrong, I want to know that I'm doing something wrong 'cause I don't want to kill somebody.'

When asked whether she had administered any medications during her shift on 28 April, Saenz said: 'I did give [Rhone] some saline, only because she said she was cramping.'

She said she opened her saline line because her nurse wasn't there. This was recorded on the patient's chart, but the patient's blood pressure didn't really go down that much, and then she said she felt nauseous.

The officers asked Saenz if she had any theories about the underlying cause of the injuries. She mentioned a 'bleach loop' and wondered whether 'our machines are hooked up and they have some bleach in them.'

She went on to explain the clinic's 'bleaching procedures' – a medicine cup was used to pour bleach into a container where it was diluted. Sponges were then soaked in the liquid and used to wipe the chairs. Although Saenz understood the policy was to use a medicine cup to measure the bleach, when pushed by the officer on whether she had ever used a syringe, Saenz acknowledged doing so.

'Sometimes I do when I can't find the little medicine cups,' she said. 'There wasn't any cups up there that day. But if you use a syringe, 10 cc, then you're going to have to, you know, put it in the receptacle. So I took my bleach and I just poured it and then I pulled up to 10 cc, 'cause I knew that would be like 10 ml.'

Other than Saenz's own statement, there was no evidence that the supply of measuring cups was depleted. Saenz further explained the monitors at the facility made her nervous, and she wanted to ensure that she was precisely following procedures.

Tests by the US Food and Drug Administration showed the presence of bleach in the dialysis lines, and the victims tested positive for bleach also. Saenz was indicted on five counts of murder and five counts of aggravated assault for the injuries to other patients. The deadly weapon Saenz used, the indictment said, was sodium hypochlorite – bleach. Even while she was out on bail, Saenz had applied for other healthcare jobs in violation of her bail conditions.

She swore an affidavit that she had no previous felony record. But documents filed by Angelina County District Attorney Clyde Herrington listed about a dozen instances of wrongdoing. They included allegations Saenz overused prescription drugs, had substance abuse and addiction problems, was fired at least four times from healthcare jobs and put false information on an employment application.

Investigators found internet searches on Saenz's computer about bleach poisoning in blood and whether bleach could be detected in dialysis lines. Saenz told the grand jury she had been concerned about the patients' deaths and looked up bleach poisoning references to see 'if this was happening, what would be the side effects'.

Saenz did not take the stand in her own defence at the trial. But a recording of the testimony she gave before a grand jury was played, where she said she felt 'railroaded' by the clinic and 'would never inject bleach into a patient'.

The defence insisted that Saenz had no motive to kill.

'Kimberly Saenz is a good nurse, a compassionate, a caring individual who assisted her patients and was well liked,' said defence attorney T. Ryan Deaton. He argued that Saenz was being targeted by the clinic's owner for faulty procedures at the facility, including improper water purification, and suggested that officials at the clinic fabricated evidence against her.

TROUBLE IN THE WORKPLACE

Before the trial, Deaton fought for the jury to have access to a US Department of Health and Human Services report from May 2008 that was heavily critical of DaVita's practices. But the report was ruled inadmissible by District Judge Barry Bryan.

According to the report, from 1 December 2007 to 28 April 2008, when Saenz had been there, the facility had 19 deaths compared to 25 for the whole of 2007. Those numbers put the facility at a mortality rate of seven per cent, which was above the state average.

The clinic was also not keeping proper records of adverse occurrences, the report stated. From 1 September 2007 to 26 April 2008, there was a total of 102 DaVita patients transported by ambulance to local hospitals during or immediately following dialysis. Of those, 60 did not have a complete adverse occurrence report.

The report went on to say that, based on record reviews and nursing staff interviews, the clinic 'did not demonstrate competence in monitoring patients during treatment alerting nurses or physicians of changes to a patient's condition and following the physician's orders for the dialysis treatment'.

However, the prosecution described claims that Saenz was being set up by her employer as 'absolutely ridiculous'. They described her as a depressed and disgruntled employee who complained about specific patients, including some of those who died or were injured.

Clinic employees reported Saenz was not happy with her employment at DaVita. Several people reported Saenz was frustrated when DaVita had reassigned her to the lesser position of patient care technician. Saenz herself considered administration of medications much less stressful and felt she was being treated unfairly by DaVita. During her shift on 28 April, Saenz was described as 'teary-eyed' in reaction to her lesser assignment.

In addition to Saenz's displeasure with her demotion, she expressed her aversion to some of the DaVita patients. One employee testified Saenz specifically voiced her dislike of Strange, Metcalf, Kelley, Few, Oates, Rhone and Risinger, all of whom either died or were injured during treatment that April. The records substantiated that during each of the alleged incidents, Saenz was at the DaVita facility functioning either as a patient care technician or as a nurse responsible for preparing medications for each patient.

TAKEN OFF THE STREETS – FOREVER

The prosecution also maintained that there were more victims, but detectives could only obtain medical waste from two weeks prior to 28 April 2008, so there was inadequate evidence to raise further indictments against Saenz. Nevertheless, an epidemiologist from the Centers for Disease Control and Prevention statistically connected Saenz to other adverse health events to patients.

'The only days there were deaths in April, she was there,' said prosecutor Clyde Herrington. 'Dialysis patients are sick, but every source of information we can find says it is very unusual for patients to die during dialysis treatment.'

He pointed out that the state did not have to prove motive to get a conviction. However, the prosecution had talked to a registered nurse who studied more than 100 healthcare killers. The most common method they used was injecting a patient with some type of medication or substance.

'Criminal behaviour is something we've been trying to understand since Cain killed Abel,' Herrington said. 'Only when the healthcare killer confesses do we know motive.'

Speculating, Herrington said he believed that Saenz was a troubled woman with marital problems who lashed out because of job dissatisfaction.

'From talking to some of the folks who worked with her, it sounded like her husband didn't want her to quit [the clinic],' Herrington said. 'She was depressed. She was frustrated, and I think she took those frustrations out on the patients.'

On 30 March 2012, Kimberly Saenz was convicted of killing five patients and deliberately injuring three others. She faced the death penalty. Addressing the jury, another of Saenz's attorneys, Steve Taylor, asked for leniency, saying: 'She's never getting out no matter what you do.'

He reminded jurors Saenz had been free on bail during the trial and prosecutors had failed to show she would present a future danger – one of the questions jurors are required to answer when deciding a death penalty.

'Society is protected,' said Taylor. 'You will never see her again.'

The prosecution made no real effort to urge the jurors to impose the death penalty.

'I know you'll reach a verdict that's just and in accordance with the law,' said Herrington after showing the jury photographs of some of the victims on a large screen in the courtroom. Ultimately, they chose to impose a life sentence for each of the murders, plus 21 years' imprisonment for each of the aggravated assaults. The Court of Appeals of Texas in San Antonio confirmed the trial court's verdict.

VIKTOR SAYENKO AND IGOR SUPRUNYUK

The Dnepropetrovsk Maniacs

IN 2007, TWO 19-YEAR-OLDS went on a three-week murder spree in Ukraine that claimed the lives of at least 21 victims. They had made videos of the murders in the hope of selling them as 'snuff' movies. They were tried alongside a third member of their gang, who committed two armed robberies.

Viktor Sayenko, Igor Suprunyuk and Alexander Hanzha went to school together in the small Red Stone district of Dnepropetrovsk, Ukraine's fourth-largest city. They banded together because they were bullied.

One of Suprunyuk's teachers said: 'The boy had a difficult character. I had the feeling that he was constantly defending himself, although no one had offended him. He was very complex, but tried not to show it. I noticed his eyes. They were blue and cold. Like icicles. They made my blood run cold.'

In the fifth grade, they would go to the local railway station and throw stones at train windows. Sayenko was arrested and his parents had to pay damages. When they discovered that Suprunyuk had been the instigator of the stone throwing, Sayenko's parents forbade him having anything more to do with Igor. But, as boys, they took no notice.

With their friend Alexander Hanzha, Viktor Sayenko and Igor Suprunyuk seized dogs off the street, hung them from trees and disembowelled them. They took photographs of each other posing beside the corpses.

Sayenko and Suprunyuk were both afraid of heights. In a weird attempt to get over this, they hung over the balustrade on the 14th floor of their apartment block for hours on end. This, apparently, had a therapeutic effect.

Hanzha was the most squeamish. He would not bathe his pet kitten in case he scalded it and had a phobia of blood. Suprunyuk suggested curing this by torturing stray dogs. Extreme cruelty to animals is often an early sign of someone who is going to turn into a serial killer.

Their grisly activities were known among their peers. Classmate Nikolai Parchuk said: 'In seventh grade, Igor Suprunyuk had a new nonsense. He decided to check whether he had enough mental strength to kill.'

The three boys seized dogs off the street and took them to a nearby wood, where they hung them from trees and disembowelled them. They took photographs of each other posing beside the corpses. These would later be used in evidence against them.

A video also showed them crucifying a kitten in a garage. They filled its mouth with glue and foam to stifle its loud mews as they nailed it to a small cross. Then they shot it. The boys were laughing and swearing, enjoying the torment of the small creature. A criminologist said he could only evaluate the video with the sound turned off.

'I could not listen to the painful squeals of puppies and kittens that were gutted alive, burned, hung up,' he said.

One photograph showed them alongside a swastika daubed on a wall with dog's blood. Their hands were raised in a Nazi salute. Suprunyuk had also painted on a toothbrush moustache, like Hitler's. He also shared his birthday, 20 April, with Hitler. An obsession with the Nazis is a frequent precursor of serial killing. However, they had not read any books about fascism, getting their knowledge about it from the internet and they outlined their gruesome philosophy in captions to their photographs: 'Kill everyone, take everything'; 'The lower you fall, the higher you will fly'; 'Killing is just a tough way of making money'.

MOVING ON TO MURDER

After graduation, Sayenko worked as a security guard, while other two were unemployed. However, Suprunyuk had been given a green Daewoo Lanos as a birthday present by his parents which he used as an unlicensed cab. At first, the three of them used it to rob passengers, but when Sayenko and Suprunyuk decided to move up to murder, Hanzha wanted out.

The first victim was a policeman who had taken his girlfriend to a recreation centre on the evening of 24 June 2007. Needing a cab, he had the misfortune to stop a green Daewoo and paid with his life.

At dawn on 26 June, the body of 33-year-old Yekaterina Ilchenko was found by her mother in a residential area of Dnepropetrovsk. She died from a blow to the head with a blunt object. Sayenko said that he and Suprunyuk had been out for a walk, innocently enough, though Suprunyuk was carrying a hammer. As Yekaterina walked past, he turned and struck her a fatal blow.

Two hours later, they saw 35-year-old Roman Tatarevich asleep on a bench. Multiple blows rained down on his head, shattering his skull and rendering him unrecognizable. The bench was opposite the public prosecutor's office.

On 1 July, Yevgenia Grischenko and Nikolai Serchuk were found murdered in the same way in the nearby town of Novomoskovsk. Their sixth victim was 14-year-old Sasha Sidak, who lived in the village of Podgorodnoye.

The police quickly realized that they had a serial killer on their hands because of the distinctive signature. They were soon at full stretch. The head of the Criminal Investigation Department Vasily

Paskalov said: 'Almost every day we found a new corpse. We didn't sleep for days and searched, searched, searched.'

There were three murders on the night of 6 July. Egor Nechvoloda, who had recently been discharged from the army, was bludgeoned to death while returning from a nightclub. His mother found his body outside their apartment block the following morning. Twenty-eight-year-old security guard Yelena Shram was walking down Kosiora Street when Suprunyuk pulled a hammer from under his shirt and struck her repeatedly. She had been carrying a bag filled with clothes, which they used to clean the hammer before throwing them away. Later Valentina Hanzha (no relation to their friend Alexander) was killed. She left three children and a disabled husband.

The following day, Andrei Sidyuk and Vadim Lyakhov, both 14, from Podgorodnoye, went fishing early in the morning. Andrei was bludgeoned to death, while Vadim fled into the woods. He told the police that there were two killers. They were standing beside a foreign car with their backs to the highway. When Vadim rode past them on his bicycle, one swung sharply and hit him painfully on the temple with something sharp. He fell off his bike, but he was able to get up run away. Andrei immediately lost consciousness.

One killer chased him on foot. The other one got into the car and started pursuing him.

But Vadim knew the area well and was able to escape. He waited for the killers to drive off and went to look for his friend. He found Andrei, lying in a pool of blood, but still breathing. Andrei tried to say something, but it was impossible to make out what it was.

Vadim bandaged Andrei's head with his shirt, put a jacket under it and went to get help. But on the nearby highway the cars sped by. Finally, one of the drivers stopped and agreed to take Andrei to the hospital, but he did not survive.

On 12 July, 48-year-old Sergei Yatsenko, who had recently survived a bout of cancer, filled up his motorcycle and went to visit his grandson. When he did not return home that night, his wife grew concerned. The family went out searching for him, later joined by the police. Four days later, his body was found near a rubbish dump.

Earlier in his life Sergei had survived when a tractor he was driving rolled into a river.

'Sergei was twice saved from certain death: first he had a terrible accident, then he underwent an oncological operation,' said his wife. 'Then he died at the hands of scum.'

On 14 July, 45-year-old Natalia Mamarchuk, a resident of the village of Diyovka, was on a motor scooter, hurrying to work at a railway station.

'Two young guys jumped out of the bushes and knocked her off her scooter,' said local resident Olga Zhuk. 'Then one of the guys took out either a hammer, or a piece of pipe, and hit Mamarchuk several times about the head. When the victim was no longer moving, the killers got on her scooter and sped off.'

Others saw what had happened. They gave chase, but could not catch them on foot.

Over the next nine days, another 12 bodies were found. Often the victims were weak and defenceless – children, pensioners, vagrants and drunks. Rumours about the maniacs abounded and the people of Dnepropetrovsk were afraid to go out at night. Some of the victims had been tortured, their bodies mutilated. Eyes were gouged out. In one particularly horrific case, the foetus was cut out of a pregnant woman.

The police now had identification sketches from Vadim Lyakhov, plus eyewitness accounts from the Mamarchuk and other attacks. Two thousand police officers were on the case, but still little progress was made. Then, on 23 July, they got a lucky break when Suprunyuk and

Sayenko went to a pawn shop to sell a mobile phone which they had stolen from one of their victims. Suprunyuk turned it on to show that it was working. The police picked up the signal and arrested the two boys. Hanzha was arrested at home trying to flush other stolen mobile phones and jewellery down the lavatory.

KILLERS WITHOUT CONSCIENCE

They were unrepentant, even confessing an earlier murder. Suprunyuk and Sayenko said they were sitting on a fence near a branch of McDonald's the previous November when they decided to rob a passing drunk. Suprunyuk hit him on the head with a stone and went through his pockets. He then decided to kill again, for the thrill of it. Picking out a passerby in the dark streets, he again struck him with a stone.

'I felt the skull burst,' he said. 'He died.'

Sayenko was equally matter-of-fact.

'On that day, 9 July 2007, Igor and I agreed to take a walk and kill someone,' he said. 'We said: "Let's go to Peschanka and kill a man there." The next day I went to accompany my girlfriend Rita to my grandmother in Tsarichanka, and then I met with Igor. I agreed to kill someone, but we spent an hour and found no one... And then a man was riding a sports bike, and we killed him.'

The victim was the chairman of one of the sports societies in Dneprodzerzhinsk, Nikolai Maryachek. They knocked him off his bike with a hammer blow to the head. After they had finished bludgeoning his face it was so disfigured that his relatives were only able to identify him by his clothes. The murderers took an expensive watch from his wrist and a camera out of his backpack.

'We still do not understand the motives,' said Mykola Kupyansky, Deputy Minister of Internal Affairs of Ukraine. 'Only in some cases, money, valuables, mobile phones were taken from the victims. Some were then thrown away. Everything was like fun or some kind of hunt.'

The pair were charged with 21 premeditated murders, four robberies, illegal possession of weapons and the cruel treatment of animals. In court they denied everything, including the videoed confessions they had made.

'They made us do it,' the two boys said. 'They wrote to us to tell us what to say, we learned this text by heart all night before being interrogated, and the video filming and photographs were simply edited and Photoshopped.'

In court, the videos of them attacking victims were shown. Caitlin Moran of *The Times* tried to watch one which was later posted on the internet. She said it showed a neatly-dressed man 'dying in unimaginable disorder and distress'.

'I do have to tell you that the man was being tortured – and not torture as shown on television dramas or films,' she wrote. 'Two similar-looking teenagers were gathered around the man, and their torture was about brutally killing someone very slowly. The footage is nearly seven minutes long. I stopped watching after 1.47.'

'There is not enough equipment in Ukraine to make such a real "cinema",' said Larissa Dovgal, representing the victims. 'In America for such a fake you would have to spend at least six months and about $10,000 for every ten seconds.'

'Do you think the blind are judging you?' asked the judge. 'We have already seen enough of you from the front and in profile.'

A classmate testified that Suprunyuk, who spoke English, had been in touch with the owner of a foreign website who wanted 'cool videos'.

'We will get rich when we kill 40 people!' he had said.

Defending his son, Sayenko's father testified that four days before his son was arrested, two men and a woman had been arrested for one of the murders. But they had powerful families and were quickly released.

'The detainees were the offspring of high-ranking persons,' he said. 'Therefore, this matter was so quickly hushed up, and instead of the guilty they substituted my son and his classmates. I also heard that the girl who had been detained at that time was already in Germany for a long time, she doesn't even have Ukrainian citizenship.'

Suprunyuk was found guilty of 21 premeditated murders, Sayenko of 18, and both were sentenced to life imprisonment. They also received 15-year sentences on the robbery charges. Hanzha, who was not involved in the killings, was found guilty of robbery and sentenced to nine years in prison.

TIAGO HENRIQUE GOMES DA ROCHA

Fury Against Everything

AT THE AGE OF 26, Brazilian serial killer Tiago Henrique Gomes da Rocha was arrested on 14 October 2014 after being pulled over by the police when riding a motorcycle carrying stolen licence plates. He then confessed to killing 39 people over just three years. Fifteen of them were young women who looked like his girlfriend who would often take him to the Assembly of God church where she was a member. His favourite modus operandi was to ride up on his motorbike, shout 'robbery', then shoot and flee without taking anything.

Rocha began killing in 2011. At first, he targeted homeless people, gay men and prostitutes. Asked why he selected these groups in particular, he said: 'Nobody would care about them.'

In 2014, he turned his attention to young women. His first female victim was 14-year-old Bárbara Costa, who had been waiting for her grandmother in a public square on 18 January when a man riding a motorcycle shot her in the chest.

The following day, 23-year-old Beatriz Moura was also shot by a man on a motorcycle. He once again didn't take anything. In all, he killed 15 women, aged between 13 and 29, in seven months. The murders took place in Goiânia, a city of 1.3 million people and the capital of Goiás state some 320 km (200 miles) from the country's capital, Brasilia.

His last victim, Ana Lidia Gomes, was also 14. He shot her dead as she left home.

It was only in August that year that the police realized that a serial killer was at work. A task force of 150 officers was formed to track him down after the families and friends of the murdered women staged a series of demonstrations to put pressure on the police and local government. They wore white and carried photographs of the victims.

Chief Police Detective Joao Gorski then told reporters: 'I believe he is a serial killer. In the beginning, he killed at random, but by the end he had established a pattern.'

UNABLE TO FIGHT THE KILLER WITHIN

Had Rocha not been caught, the murders would have continued. Even the Sunday before he was arrested, he had tried to kill a woman but was foiled when his gun failed to go off. The woman later identified him as her would-be assassin.

Interviewed by the newspaper *Folha de São Paulo*, he said he regretted his crimes but had been 'moved by a greater power'. Rocha also said he killed because of the 'fury he felt against everything', which only subsided when he murdered.

'I wanted to say that I am remorseful, that I wanted to have a chance to pay for what I've done – to ask for forgiveness,' he told *Folha*.

During the interview Rocha sat with his eyes downcast, pausing frequently and giving short answers. He avoided personal questions but confirmed that he had problems in his childhood. He was asked twice about the number of victims. The first time he refused to answer. The second time, he said only: 'No comment.'

Nor could he explain why he killed so many people, simply saying: 'It was stronger than me, I can't explain,' adding that he was feeling 'bad, very bad' about the killings. *Folha* reported that he would often drink before the killings to give himself courage. He also dehumanized his victims in his mind's eye. When speaking to the police, he would refer to them only by number in the order that he had killed them.

'All the police officers who followed the interrogation were shocked by his coldness, not only with his modus operandi but also in the way he formulated his ideas,' said the chief interrogator, Commissioner Douglas Pedrosa, of the Goiás Civil Police. 'He identified each victim by a number – number 30, number 12.'

Asked for the name of the first woman he had murdered, he answered: 'It wasn't a woman. It was a man.'

According to the police, victim number one was 16-year-old Diego Martins Mendes. In 2011, Rocha approached Diego at a bus station, believing him to be gay. He then lured the youth into undergrowth with the promise of sex. The act was never consummated, according to Rocha. Instead, he strangled Diego. His body was never found.

Rocha's next victims were two more men. One was a former co-worker, who he stabbed. The other was a man who Rocha again thought was gay.

However, Commissioner Pedrosa said Rocha remembered every detail of his many crimes with relish.

'After admitting to a murder, he would stay there for some five minutes in a catatonic state,' Pedroso said. Rocha told police he was thinking about the crime – reliving it, even. At times, he would have a smile on his face.

'After, he would give details about the place and what he was feeling,' Pedrosa said. But he was not thinking about the victim, only the action he had taken. 'He didn't have details of the faces, he had details of the violence.'

Asked what motivated him to kill, he simply said: 'I am angry with the world.'

As well as being cold during interrogation, he was visibly bothered by female police staff. When a woman walked in he 'stopped talking, said he was bothered and that he wasn't going to talk anymore,' Pedrosa said.

Nevertheless, he was determined to get things off his chest. When his lawyer, Thiago Vidal, counselled him about his right to remain silent, Rocha pounded his fists on the interrogation table and insisted: 'No, I will talk. I have to get this from inside me.'

Vidal said he was concerned that the police were applying undue pressure and left the interview room 'perplexed'.

'At first I thought the police may have coerced him into confessing to a crime he didn't commit, but he narrated with richness of detail each of the deaths,' the lawyer told *Folha*.

While Rocha talked, the lawyer read through the police report detailing the confession from the previous two days. There were no discrepancies in his retelling of his grisly tale.

'He didn't hesitate,' Vidal said. 'Everything fits.'

In jail, Rocha attempted suicide using shards from a light bulb. He was put on suicide watch and kept in handcuffs.

Police chief Eduardo Prado said: 'We're monitoring him constantly. He doesn't love himself and he's already attempted suicide. He constantly asks for dental floss when I'm with him. When you ask him if it's so he can kill himself, he just laughs sarcastically.'

At his request, Rocha was visited by his mother, an aunt and four other relatives. They described him as a quiet young man with few friends. He lived with his mother and a brother, and rarely went out to social events at night. He had never met his father.

After graduating from high school, he worked for a couple of years in a private security firm, from where he stole the .38-calibre revolver that he used in the murders. The gun was found at his mother's home. Police confirmed that the gun was linked to the murders of six women that year. In the four months before he was arrested, Rocha had worked a night security shift in a large hospital in Goiânia.

Although Rocha said he felt remorseful about his crimes, his arrest had not sated his appetite for killing. In jail, he asked the police guarding his cell if he was allowed to murder other inmates.

Police chief Prado, one of those in charge of the investigation into the slayings, said: 'He asked whether he would face trial if he killed someone else in custody. He still wants to kill. We found this attitude very strange, as well as the disjointed things he's always saying.'

A DIFFICULT MAN TO MANAGE

His behaviour continued to puzzle his captors. During the early hours of the morning he read 40 magazines from back to front in quick succession.

'It was a curious thing that he would read from the back forwards and very quickly, as if it were a task he was being made to do, reading aloud,' said Prado. But that did not lull his jailers into a false sense of security. 'Truly, when he is transferred to a long-term prison, that prison's management will have to have a very robust and more methodical control of the situation, which is actually highly dangerous.'

After a week in custody, Rocha began to open up. He said his rage started when he was sexually abused as an 11-year-old boy. That was when his urge to kill began.

'I had an ordinary childhood until I was 11. Then I was sexually abused by a neighbour,' he said. 'After that I felt like I was nothing. In a way I'm a victim here, too.'

His rage grew through his adolescence. When he reached adulthood, it peaked.

'When I was 22, I couldn't stop myself anymore. It was like I had to do it,' he said. That was when he killed his first victim – a homeless person.

Soon, he started targeting women and girls.

'I was rejected a lot in the past, so I directed part of my anger towards women,' he said.

The killings were random. Rocha said he shot many of his victims while speeding past them on his motorcycle. Some of the women were walking home when he shot them. Others were waiting at bus stops, he said.

'My mind went blank, but I would cry later,' he said, noting that he was emotionless when he randomly selected his targets.

He also admitted stabbing prostitutes and robbing stores. Footage from one stickup in a shop had helped police identify him.

Although Rocha's lawyers still insisted he had confessed to crimes he didn't commit after police interrogated him aggressively, Rocha confirmed that he was the killer in interviews with the media.

'I want to ask forgiveness,' he said.

Speaking to Brazil's *Jornal Nacional* news programme on TV Globo, Rocha said he was motivated by 'a great anger' and that killing was the only way to get it out of his system.

'I tried to do other things to get it out, but they didn't work,' he said. 'When the thing comes you have to do it. There's no way of explaining it.'

Speaking at a news conference, Chief of Police Deusny Aparecido said Rocha 'felt anger at everything and everyone. He had no link to any of his victims and chose them at random. It could have been me, you or your children.'

Despite his confession, Rocha was tried separately for each murder. The first conviction came on 16 February 2016. It was for the murder of 15-year-old student Ana Karla Lemes da Silva, who was shot in the chest. He was sentenced to 20 years.

On 2 March 2016 he was convicted of the murder of 22-year-old administrative assistant Juliana Neubia Dias. The young woman was killed while in a car with her boyfriend and a friend. Sentence: 20 years.

The third conviction, for another 20 years, was for the murder of 17-year-old Ana Rita de Lima. Then 20 more for the murder of 16-year-old student Arlete dos Anjos Carvalho. Then he got 22 years for the murder of 15-year-old Carla Barbosa Araújo in front of her older sister.

The murder of 14-year-old Bárbara Luíza Ribeiro Costa, shot in the chest while sitting in a car, earned him another 25 years. A further 25 years was handed down for the murder of 51-year-old photographer Mauro Nunes. During the sentence, the victim's son landed two punches on the defendant. Yet another 25 years was given for shooting 13-year-old Taynara Rodrigues da Cruz in the back.

Fourteen-year-old student Ana Lidia Gomes was shot four times on 2 August 2014 at a bus stop on her way to meet her mother. Sentence: 26 years. Twenty-three-year-old butcher Adailton dos Santos Farias was murdered in July 2014. Sentence: 25 years. Twenty-four-year-old journalist Janaína Nicácio de Souza was murdered in a bar. Sentence: 25 years and six months. Twenty-eight-year-old housewife Lilian Sissi was murdered as she left to pick up her children from school. Another 25 years.

The jail time continued to mount, month by month, until his 33rd trial on 20 September 2018, when Tiago Henrique Gomes da Rocha was sentenced to 21 years in prison for the murder of 26-year-old receptionist Bruna Gleycielle de Souza Gonçalves, who was killed at a bus stop on 8 May 2014. Altogether, the sentences came to more than 600 years.

In addition to the killings, the court sentenced him to 12 years and four months for twice robbing the same lottery agency. He was also sentenced to three years in prison for the illegal possession of a gun. On appeal this was reduced to a fine and a term of community service, though it is not clear how he will find the time to do that.

BRUCE GEORGE PETER LEE

Firestarter

ONE OF BRITAIN'S MOST prolific serial killers, Bruce Lee had 26 deaths to his name by the time he was 19. Pleading guilty to multiple counts of manslaughter, he said: 'I am devoted to fire... Fire is my master, that is why I cause these fires.'

Over the course of six years, there had been a series of fatal fires in Hull, north-east England. Although people had died, there was no suspicion of wrongdoing. All of them were thought to have been started by accident. Then, on 4 December 1979, there was a fire at a family home claiming three lives that was certainly arson.

In the early hours 34-year-old Edith Hastie woke to find her home at 12 Selby Street ablaze. Fortunately, her three daughters were staying with relatives and friends, but her four sons were in the house. She woke 15-year-old Charlie. Together they tried to rescue nine-year-old Thomas, who suffered from muscular dystrophy, but were beaten back by smoke and flames.

With flames coming up the stairs, Charlie pushed his mother out of the first-floor window, then went back to try and rescue his younger brothers Paul and Peter, who were 12 and eight. By the time the fire brigade arrived, the three boys had suffered 80 per cent burns and died later, while Thomas escaped with relatively minor injuries.

When Detective Superintendent Ronald Sagar arrived to investigate he found two spent matches outside the front door and the area smelt of paraffin. Crime scene investigators found that paraffin had been poured through the letter box, followed by a lighted newspaper. The house fire was now a murder case.

The Hasties were well-known to the police. The father of the house, Tommy, was in jail for burglary. His children were vandals and petty thieves. They were hated by everyone in the neighbourhood. There was no shortage of people who held a grudge against them. Some months earlier, a piece of cardboard snipped from a cereal packet had been pushed through the door. On it was a note addressed to: 'A family of f***ing rubbish.'

It read: 'We all hate you, you should all live on an island. (Devils Island) But I's not kidding but I promised you a bomb and by hell I'm not kidding. Why don't you flit while you've got the chance. We can't get you out normally then we'll bastard well bomb you and that's too good for you.'

It was soon discovered that the handwriting matched that of a frail old lady who lived nearby and had been terrorized by the Hastie boys. She was an unlikely murderer and the investigation soon stalled.

After six months, Sagar decided to interview local homosexuals who used a public lavatory nearby as a pick-up point. He called them all in on one day and accused each in turn on the off chance that one of them would confess.

'It was a bluff,' he said. But it paid off. Nineteen-year-old Bruce George Peter Lee admitted starting the fire.

'I didn't mean to kill them,' he said.

A DIFFICULT START IN LIFE

The son of a prostitute, Lee suffered from epilepsy and was disabled. He walked with a limp and his right arm folded across his chest. As a result, other kids teased him. Born Peter Dinsdale, he changed his name in homage to the martial arts movie star, Bruce Lee. Known locally as 'Daft Peter', the self-confessed arsonist had been brought up in children's homes. He had a low IQ and worked as a labourer.

Lee told the police that he had started the fire to get back at Charlie Hastie, who had encouraged him into acts of gross indecency and threatened to go to the police, as he was still a minor, unless Lee gave him money. Furthermore, Lee had fallen for Charlie's 16-year-old sister Angie, who despised him.

He told Sagar that he hadn't meant to kill anyone but set fire to Charlie's house 'to give him a real frightener'. He described in detail how he had poured paraffin through the letter box, then tried to light it with a match. When that failed, he lit a newspaper and stuffed it through the letter box.

Six months earlier, another house in the neighbourhood caught fire one night. There had been no fatalities, but 27-year-old Rosabell Fenton and her seven-year-old daughter Samantha had suffered severe burns. Mrs Fenton was pregnant at the time and lost the child. She reported seeing Daft Peter outside the house and thought she had seen his hand appear through the letter box. However, there had been no inquest and the cause of the fire was thought to have been a cigarette dropped on the carpet earlier.

In custody, Lee admitted causing this fire, too, though he could provide no motive.

'I just did it,' he said. 'Someone I knew didn't like her and, well, I just did it.'

Asked if he was an habitual firestarter, he said: 'I like fires, I do. I like fires.'

After a pause, he said: 'I killed a baby once.'

He described climbing through the window of a house in West Dock Avenue a few years earlier, sprinkling paraffin around the living

Bruce George Peter Lee changed his name in homage to his favourite martial arts movie star. He had a low IQ and worked as a labourer.

room and setting fire to it. Six-month-old Katrina Thacker, who was asleep in her cot upstairs, died. At the time, no foul play was suspected.

Lee admitted that he'd had a falling-out with the family. Then he said: 'I've done more... there's four other fires with one dead in each one.'

The first was in 1973. Six-year-old Richard Ellerington had been at the same special needs school as Lee. He had been trapped in a bedroom when the rest of the household escaped. The cause of the fire was thought to have been a faulty gas cooker.

The morning after the fire, the school bus stopped outside Richard Ellerington's house as usual. Lee was on board.

'When we stopped in the bus next morning,' Lee told Sagar, 'they said he's died in a fire during night. I just sat on bus quiet, looking out a window and said nowt... I've kept [it] secret from everybody for years.'

Again, he could provide no motive.

The death toll mounted dramatically when Lee claimed to have set fire to an old people's home in 1977, resulting in the deaths of 11 elderly men. They had been trapped on the second floor. The blame was erroneously placed on a plumber who had been using a blowtorch earlier that day on a pipe in the boiler room.

That was directly below the room where the fire had started. However, experts found that there were no faults with the plumber's work or his tools and the plumber himself vehemently denied any errors on his part.

To check out the veracity of Lee's confession, Sagar put him in a police car and got Lee to direct the driver to the Wensley Lodge residential home which had been gutted on 5 January 1977, just three days after the fire at West Dock Avenue. The Lodge was just a few miles from Lee's home. He had cycled there with a can of paraffin balanced on his handlebars. The target was picked at random.

'I just come along there to do a big house, just ride along, any house,' he said.

Picking Wensley Lodge, he had kicked in a window, spread paraffin around and set fire to it. He learnt later that he had killed 11 'old blokes' when he read about the fire in the newspaper. At 16, he was already a mass murderer.

A BURNING DESIRE FOR FIRE

In fact, his career as an arsonist had begun at the age of nine when he had set fire to a timber yard. Sometime after he had set fire to a shopping precinct, causing £17,000 of damage. He told Sagar: 'I know when I'm going to start a fire because my fingers tingle,' adding more chillingly: 'I am devoted to fire and despise people.'

There were more confessions. Four months after the murder of Richard Ellerington, Lee was out on the streets again with a can of paraffin. Around 6 am, he noticed a house in Glasgow Street with a broken front window. He climbed in. In the front room 72-year-old recluse Arthur Smythe was asleep. Gangrene in his legs stopped him going out. Lee doused the room with paraffin, set it on fire and walked out of the front door. Smythe stood no chance. An overturned paraffin heater was thought to have been to blame. The pensioner also lit a candle to provide light when the electricity was cut off.

Two weeks later, Lee had threatened to kill pigeons belonging to a boy called Shaun Lister. Thirty-four-year-old David Brewer threatened to clout him if he did. Two days after, Brewer fell asleep on the sofa and awoke to find himself on fire. Incapacitated by a work injury, he was unable to flee. Shaun's mother Hilda doused him in wet towels, but he died in hospital eight days later. Although the fire damage was confined to the settee and the surrounding floor it was concluded that Brewer had been drying clothes by the fire and they had caught alight. Soon after, Shaun's pigeons were found dead, their necks wrung.

Over a year later, on 23 December 1973, 82-year-old Elizabeth Rokahr was found dead of smoke inhalation. She had poor eyesight and could only walk with a frame. It was concluded that she had been smoking in bed and the sheets had caught fire. Six years later, Lee admitted entering her home and setting fire to it. Once again, he could provide no motive.

Seventy-seven-year-old Dorothy Stevenson was babysitting her great-grandchildren on 3 June 1976. She was coming downstairs after putting one-year-old Andrew Edwards to bed when she saw smoke coming out of the cupboard under the stairs. Quickly, she took five-year-old David Edwards and his sister to neighbours. It was only then that she remembered Andrew. It was too late to get back to him and the child died. It was thought that David must had started the fire by playing with matches, though his parents insisted that there were no matches in the house. Lee later admitted sneaking into the house and pouring paraffin under the stairs to set it on fire. The elderly Mrs Stevenson was so traumatized by the incident that she was committed to a mental hospital.

Just three months after the fire at Wensley Lodge, Lee claimed two more lives. On 27 April 1977, Peter Jordan and his two children were staying with his friends Albert and Gwendoline Gold and their two children. Jordan was sleeping on the sofa when he awoke to find the living room on fire. He raced upstairs to warn the others. Albert Gold suffered severe burns trying to rescue the children. Two got out. But seven-year-old Mark Gold had gone back to try and rescue 13-year-old Deborah Jordan, who was mentally incapacitated. Peter Jordan was accused of leaving a lighted cigarette in an ashtray. However, he had noticed that a window near an outside door had been broken. This was how Lee had got in.

On 6 January the following year, 24-year-old Christine Dickson had left her four children in her front room while she visited her next-door neighbour Kathleen Hartley. Christine's husband was ill in bed upstairs. When she returned, the windows were blackened with smoke.

She rushed inside to rescue her baby Bryan and handed him to Mrs Hartley, then raced back in to get Mark, Steven and Michael, who were four, three and 17 months. Mrs Hartley saw a ring of fire rise from the floor to envelop them. The inquest concluded that the children had been playing with lighter fluid, though Mr Dickson, who escaped, said there was none in the house. Lee said that he had been stalking the streets with a washing-up liquid bottle filled with paraffin, which he sprayed through the letter box, followed by a lighted paper. By then he had killed 23 people.

Psychiatric evaluations pronounced Lee sane and fit to stand trial. On 20 January 1981, he pleaded not guilty at Leeds Crown Court to 26 counts of murder. Instead, he pleaded guilty to 26 counts of manslaughter on the grounds of diminished responsibility, along with 11 counts of arson where life was endangered. Prosecuting counsel Gerald Coles said the Crown was prepared to accept his manslaughter pleas, saying of Lee: 'The fires were his only true achievement in life.'

The judge recommended that Lee be detained in a maximum-security mental hospital indefinitely for the protection of the public. Although the death toll of 26 made him the most prolific serial killer in British history, the case was overshadowed by that of Peter Sutcliffe, the Yorkshire Ripper, who had been arrested on 2 January that same year.

After the trial, the *Sunday Times* published a series of articles questioning some of the convictions – given his physical disabilities it seemed unlikely that Lee could have performed some of the actions outlined in his confessions. However, the defence were only given leave to appeal on the Wensley Lodge manslaughters, which were overturned. Nevertheless, it is unlikely that Lee will ever be released.

LARRY EYLER

The Interstate Killer

LARRY EYLER WAS KNOWN as the Interstate Killer or the Highway Killer because he dumped his victims' bodies along the interstate highways from south-east Wisconsin to north Kentucky. They were young men who had been sexually abused before being strangled or stabbed repeatedly. Often, they had been bound and sometimes their bodies had been mutilated or dismembered. After Eyler's conviction for just one of his numerous murders, the judge said: 'If there ever was a person the death penalty is appropriate for, it is you. You are an evil person. You truly deserve to die for your acts.'

The crimes were spread out across a number of jurisdictions, so he had killed at least ten men before the police realized that a serial killer was at work. The perpetrator was clearly gay. Although homosexuality was largely decriminalized at the time, it was not widely accepted in the Midwest. This meant that the police were not trusted by the gay community, allowing the killer to go about his monstrous business with impunity.

THERE'S A KILLER ON THE ROAD

Eyler's first known victim was 19-year-old Steven Crockett, whose mutilated corpse was found in a cornfield outside Kankakee, Illinois, 64 km (40 miles) south of Chicago on 23 October 1982. He had been stabbed 32 times – four times in the head – and had been dead for 12 hours when discovered.

Larry Eyler was told by the judge: 'You are an evil person. You truly deserve to die for your acts.'

Then on Christmas Day 1982, the body of barman John R. Johnson was found 56 km (35 miles) away near Lowell, Indiana. He had gone missing from Chicago's seedy Uptown district a week after Crockett had been killed, but the police in Illinois and Indiana had no reason to think that the two crimes were related. The FBI's Violent Criminal Apprehension Program (ViCAP), which records and correlates information on violent crime, was not begun until 1985.

The following day, a 26-year-old named Edgar Underkofler disappeared from Rantoul, Illinois. His body was not discovered until 4 March 1983, in a field close to Danville, Illinois. His shoes had been removed and he was wearing white socks which were not his.

On 28 December 1982, two more mutilated bodies were found in Indiana. Twenty-three-year-old Steven Agan had left his mother's home in Terre Haute on 19 December to go and see a movie. He did not return. His body was found 48 km (30 miles) away in a wooded area outside Newport in Vermillion County, close to Indiana State Road 63. His throat had been slashed and there were more frenzied cuts across the abdomen and chest as if the killer wanted to open him up. In more than ten years in forensic pathology, Dr John Pless at Bloomington House said he had never seen such mutilation.

It did not seem that Agan had been killed where the body was found. At an abandoned farm nearby, traces of his flesh were found on nails hammered into the wall. Police speculated that Agan had been hung upside down and cut open like a deer being dressed. Like Underkofler, who was found later, he was wearing white socks that were not his.

The same day, Dr Pless had to perform another autopsy, on 21-year-old John Roach from Indianapolis whose body had been dumped along Interstate Highway 70 in Putnam County some 48 km (30 miles) from his home. He had disappeared three days before Christmas and had been the victim of a frenzied knife attack. Pless noted similarities between the three Indiana cases and called the state police to suggest a central investigation, rather than leaving the matter separately to the local police. They ignored his advice.

Two days later, 22-year-old David Block, who had just graduated from Yale, disappeared while visiting his parents in Chicago. His Volkswagen was found locked on the Tri-State Tollway near Deerfield to the north of the city. When his skeletal remains were found near Zionsville, Indiana, some 240 km (150 miles) to the south, on 7 May 1984, decomposition and exposure to the elements made it impossible to determine the cause of death.

While the police still refused to link these cases, Indianapolis' gay newspaper *The Works* set up a hotline and published a profile of the killer.

'This man is not openly gay yet,' it said, 'but he knows that he is, and when the urge hits him he can only absolve this tendency by committing a murder.'

Even when the police did take an interest, the clientele of gay bars were suspicious and refused to co-operate.

On the night 21 March 1982, 26-year-old Jay Reynolds, the owner of a Baskin-Robbins ice-cream shop in Lexington, Kentucky, had left his wife and nine-week-old son to close up his store. The next day, his body was found at the bottom of an embankment alongside US Highway 25, south of the city. He had been stabbed to death.

On 8 April 1983, the body of 28-year-old Gustavo Herrera was found buried under debris on a building site. A father of two, he often hung out in gay bars. His right hand had been cut off and was found nearby. A week later, the body of 16-year-old Ervin Gibson was found with the corpse of a dog covered with rubbish and branches in woods a couple of miles west of the Herrera dump site. His overalls had been pulled down and he had been stabbed numerous times. Both bodies had been found near exit ramps from I-94.

The body of 18-year-old Jimmy Roberts, a Chicagoan, was found floating in a creek to the south of the city on 9 May. His trousers had been pulled down and he had been stabbed more than 30 times. However, the police did not associate it with the other killings because none of the previous victims had been found in water, nor had any of them been black.

That same day the body of Daniel Scott McNieve was found in a field in Henderson County on State Road 39, a mile south of I-70. It was taken to Bloomington Hospital where Dr Pless recognized the handiwork of the killer of Steven Agan and John Roach. He drew this to the attention of the state police who, this time, took notice.

The Central Indiana Multi-Agency Investigative Team was set up under Lieutenant Jerry Campbell. A force of 50 officers compiled a list of unsolved murders of young men and boys. By 6 June, they had a suspect. A caller from Indianapolis had named 31-year-old Larry Eyler. Years before, on 3 August 1978, Eyler had picked up hitchhiker Mark Henry near Terre Haute. Pulling into a dark side street, he pulled a butcher's knife and forced Henry to strip. He handcuffed him, but Henry broke away. Eyler pursued him and stabbed him through the lung. Henry played dead and, after Eyler had gone, found refuge in a nearby house.

After the police and medics had turned up, Eyler gave himself up, handing over the keys to the handcuffs. He was arrested and, in his pickup, the police found a sword, three knives, a whip and a canister of tear gas. Eyler was bailed and charges were dropped after he gave $2,500 compensation to Henry and paid $43 in court costs.

Three years later, Eyler was arrested for drugging a 14-year-old boy and dumping him in a coma in the woods near Greencastle, Indiana. The boy survived and his parents dropped charges when he left the hospital after several days with no lasting damage.

BUILDING A PROFILE

Born in Crawfordsville, Indiana, in 1952, Eyler had a difficult early life. His father was an alcoholic who used to beat his wife and children.

Larry's parents split when he was two. His mother remarried three times, each time to an abusive alcoholic. Eyler spent some time in a children's home. As an adolescent he came out as gay, though he still tried dating girls. On the gay scene, it was noted that he had a sadistic streak and a violent temper.

He failed to graduate from high school and dropped out of college. Working as a decorator and a liquor store clerk in Greencastle, Indiana, on Saturdays, he lived supposedly platonically in a condominium in Terre Haute with a 40-year-old library science professor named Robert David Little, who he'd met in 1975. He also had a long-term masochistic relationship with John Dobrovolskis who lived with his wife Sally, two children and three foster children in Greenview, Illinois. Dobrovolskis' wife tolerated her husband's sexual aberrance and Eyler often lodged with them on weekdays, paying a third of the rent. He also drove to Chicago to visit the gay scene there.

With no other suspect, the Indiana police concentrated their surveillance on Eyler. While they followed him, the skeletal remains of another victim, found in Ford County, Illinois, on 2 July 1983, was added to the list.

On the night of 30 August 1983, 28-year-old Ralph Carlisle left his girlfriend in Chicago's Uptown and went out on the town. The following day, his body was found in Lake Forest, near where Gustavo Herrera and Ervin Gibson had been discovered that April. His trousers had been pulled down and he had been stabbed in the torso 17 times, practically disembowelling him. There were handcuff marks on his wrists and the killer had left footprints.

Carlisle had lived just two doors down from Herrera, while Crockett and Johnson lived not far away. The Illinois police realized that they had a serial killer on their hands. Reviewing their files, they came across the case of Craig Townsend who had been abducted from Uptown on 12 October 1982, and was found drugged, beaten and dumped semi-conscious near Lowell, Indiana. This led the Illinois police to join the Indiana task force. FBI psychologists then came up with a psychological profile of the killer that fitted Eyler.

The Chicago police were now on the lookout for Eyler and spotted him cruising Uptown on 30 September 1983. He picked up Daryl Hayward, offering him $100 for sex – specifically bondage. However, the tail lost him when he drove south on I-90 into Lake County, Indiana.

Near Lowell, Eyler stopped and persuaded Hayward to have sex with him in an abandoned yard. They were making their way back to Eyler's pickup when State Trooper Kenneth Buehrle stopped to issue a ticket for parking illegally beside the state highway. When Buehrle radioed in Eyler's details, he was told to arrest him.

Once in custody, Eyler was charged with soliciting for prostitution. It was also noticed that the soles of his boots resembled plaster casts taken from the Carlisle crime scene. A bloodstained knife was found in his pickup. Nevertheless, he was released.

The investigation continued, though. Handcuffs were found in Little's apartment. Phone records led the police to Dobrovolskis' home. Eyler was there. Questioned by the police, he explained their unconventional relationship and admitted that he liked to bind his partners before sex.

Then a dismembered corpse, drained of blood, was found near Highway 31 at Petrified Springs Park, in Kenosha County, Wisconsin. It proved to be that of 18-year-old Eric Hansen, a street hustler from St Francis, Wisconsin, last seen alive in Milwaukee on 27 September. An identified skeleton was found in Jasper County, Indiana, on 15 October. Notches on the bones showed the victim had been stabbed.

Four days later four more bodies were found on a deserted farm near Lake Village, Indiana. Detectives found a pentagram and an inverted cross inside the abandoned building. Two were identified as

22-year-old Michael Bauer and 19-year-old John Bartlett. The other two remain unidentified.

Surviving victims came forward. Ed Healey from West Virginia said that Eyler had handcuffed him for sex, then beat him and threatened him with a shotgun, while Jim Griffin from Chicago said that Eyler had beaten him and threatened him with a knife. Forensic evidence was also mounting, with blood found on Eyler's boots and knife matching Carlisle's blood type, though DNA fingerprinting was not available then. But at a preliminary hearing on 23 January 1984, Eyler's attorney David Schippers managed to get the bulk of the evidence ruled as inadmissible and Eyler was released.

On 21 August 1984, the janitor of an apartment house on West Sherman Street, Chicago, found the building's dumpster full of bin bags containing body parts. A witness recalled seeing Eyler, who lived at 1618 West Sherman, putting rubbish bags into the dumpster that night. Fingerprints were found, along with blood and more bin bags in his apartment. The body belonged to 16-year-old Daniel Bridges. A male prostitute from the age of 12, he had been bound to a chair before being beaten and raped, then stabbed to death. Eyler had then dismembered Bridges' body in his bathroom.

When the case finally came to court on 1 July 1986, Eyler pleaded not guilty. He was convicted of murdering Bridges and sentenced to death by lethal injection. He also got 15 years in prison for aggravated kidnapping and five years for attempting to conceal his victim's death. Appeals dragged on for another three years.

Eyler admitted another 20 murders, receiving a further 60 years on each count. He also testified against Robert Little, who he said was his accomplice in the murder and mutilation of Steven Agan. Little was acquitted. Eyler died in jail on 6 March 1994 from complications related to AIDS.

RANDALL WOODFIELD

The I-5 Bandit

No one expected things to turn out badly for Randy Woodfield. At high school in Newport, Oregon, he got good grades and was the star of the football team there and at Portland State University (PSU), even trying out for the Green Bay Packers. Yet he ended up in jail for life for murder, with another 90 years for a string of other crimes. And that's not to mention the other murders and felonies he no doubt committed but was never prosecuted for – the authorities reasoned that they had their man, and didn't need to waste further time and public money in court.

Born in 1950 in Salem, Oregon, to a middle-class family, Woodfield seems to have been overshadowed by his two older sisters – one who became a doctor, the other an attorney. Nevertheless, everything seemed set fair for young Randy until he was 11, when he began exposing himself to women. He also had anger issues, but the therapists his parents employed found they couldn't help him. At college he joined the Campus Crusade for Christ and the Fellowship of Christian Athletes. But the flashing continued and he graduated to petty theft and burglary. It was hoped that he would grow out of it. He didn't.

Meanwhile, his misdemeanours were covered up to keep him in the football team. Things got more difficult when he was arrested for breaking into a girlfriend's apartment and trashing her bedroom in 1970. Three years later, he got a suspended sentence for indecent exposure. The Packers sent him home after a series of similar offences.

HE HAD IT ALL, BUT IT WASN'T ENOUGH

In 1975, a man carrying a knife forced women to perform oral sex on him before stealing their handbags. Policewomen were sent out as bait and on 3 March Randy Woodfield was arrested after stealing marked money from one of the officers. He served four years of a ten-year sentence.

Though he had trouble holding down a job – and holding on to a girlfriend – Woodfield was still brimming with self-confidence. He was seen cruising around Portland in a gold 1974 'Champagne Edition' Volkswagen Beetle and took unmistakable pride in his physique. He was especially fond of sending naked photos of himself to women. In late 1979, Woodfield was photographed with his muscles abundantly oiled for inclusion in *Playgirl* magazine.

The year following his release, his former classmate 29-year-old Cherie Ayers was raped and murdered, having been savagely beaten around the head and stabbed in the neck. They had met up at a class reunion and Woodfield was an immediate suspect. During interrogation, detectives found his answers 'evasive' and 'deceptive'. Although the semen found on the victim did not match his blood type, subsequent DNA analysis proved a link. By then Woodfield was incarcerated for life. He was also linked to the murders of Darcey Fix and Doug Altic, who had been shot dead in Altic's apartment. Woodfield had a connection to the murdered woman. One of his closest friends – a teammate from PSU's track team – had dated Fix. Again, Woodfield was questioned, but police had nothing concrete tying him to the murders.

On 9 December 1980, a young man wearing a false beard held up a petrol station in Vancouver. Four nights later, a man answering the same description held up an ice-cream parlour in Eugene, Oregon. The next night he robbed a drive-in restaurant in Albany. A week later, he robbed a chicken restaurant in Seattle, forcing a waitress to masturbate him in a toilet cubicle. Twenty minutes later, he robbed another ice-cream parlour. The culprit quickly became known as the I-5 Bandit as the crimes were taking place up and down Interstate 5, which runs parallel to the Pacific coast for 2,250 km (1,400 miles) from the Canadian to the Mexican borders, through Washington state, Oregon and California. All of the I-5 Bandit's crimes took place close to interstate exits.

He hit a Vancouver petrol station a second time on 8 January 1981. This time, after he had emptied the till, he forced the attendant to expose her breasts. Four days later, he wounded a woman grocery clerk with gunfire in Sutherlin, Oregon. Two days after that, still wearing a false beard, he broke into a home in Corvallis, Oregon, where he forced two sisters, aged eight and ten, to strip and fellate him.

Four days later, he raped two women, Shari Hull and Beth Wilmot, in an office building, then shot them in the back of the head as they lay face down. Beth somehow survived. On 26 and 29 January, he committed robberies in Eugene, Medford and Grant's Pass, during which he fondled a female customer and a clerk.

On 3 February 1981, 37-year-old Donna Eckard and her 14-year-old stepdaughter Jannell Jarvis were raped and murdered together in bed at their home in Mountain Gate, California. Jannell had also been sodomized. The same day, a female clerk was kidnapped, raped and sodomized after a holdup in nearby Redding. The next day, an identical crime was reported in Yreka. The bandit went on to rob a motel in Ashland the same night. A fabric store in Corvallis was hit five days later, where the bandit molested the clerk and her customer before departing. He also committed three more sexual assaults on 12 February during robberies in Vancouver, Olympia and Bellevue, Washington.

The I-5 Bandit struck again in Eugene on 18 and 21 February, with another sexual assault in Corvallis on 25 February. But by then the police were on his tail after former girlfriend Julie Reitz was found dead at her home in Beaverton, Oregon, on 15 February.

Woodfield had organized a Valentine's Day party at the Marriott Hotel in downtown Portland. No one showed up. At 2 am, Woodfield

Randall Woodfield was drafted by the NFL to play for the Green Bay Packers, but they had to let him go after a series of arrests for indecent exposure.

turned up on Reitz's doorstep a few miles away. They had a glass of wine and were about to have a cup of coffee when he raped and shot her. Her mother found her body at the bottom of the stairs at 8.30 am. Woodfield had been working as a bouncer at the Faucet Tavern in Raleigh Hills where he let the 18-year-old in with a fake ID. 'Randy was fired from the bar,' said his colleague Chuck Heath later. 'His thing was young girls. He was always bringing underage girls into the place. Then he asked me to go with him to small claims court and lie. I realized he was kind of weird.'

TRIED, CONDEMNED, INCARCERATED – AND UNREPENTANT

Detective Dave Kominek of the sheriff's office in Marion County, Oregon, was working on the murder of Shari Hull. He quickly put a case together against Woodfield. Having already served a prison sentence for preying on women, Woodfield was acquainted with some of the victims and he matched the physical description provided by witnesses. Then Marion County detectives put together a payphone call log that showed Woodfield using phonecards to make calls within a few miles of various murders.

One survivor, 21-year-old Lisa Garcia, then picked his photograph out of a lineup. When his apartment was searched, tape of the same brand as that used to bind the victims was found. In his racquetball bag, there was a spent .32 bullet that matched those found in the victims.

On 9 March 1981, Randall Woodfield was charged with Hull's murder, Garcia's attempted murder and two counts of sodomy. Woodfield, employing a public defender, entered a plea of not guilty. A week later, indictments were rolling in from various jurisdictions in Washington and Oregon, including multiple counts of murder, rape, sodomy, attempted kidnapping, armed robbery and possession of a firearm by an ex-convict.

In the summer of 1981, Woodfield went on trial in the Hull and Garcia cases. Lisa Garcia testified against him. The prosecutor Chris Van Dyke (son of actor Dick Van Dyke) said he was ready with 'armloads of evidence, overwhelming evidence'. He also characterized the accused as 'an arrogant, cold, unemotional individual... probably the coldest, most detached defendant I've ever seen'.

The flimsy defence alleged mistaken identity, even suggesting that Garcia had identified Woodfield because she had been hypnotized by a detective. Woodfield eventually took the stand. He spoke softly, standing with his arms crossed. Crime writer Ann Rule, then a reporter, said: 'Randy Woodfield had been touted in the media as a massively muscled professional athlete. The man in person seemed strangely diminished, not a superman after all.... He looked, if anything, humbled – a predatory creature brought down and caged in mid-rampage.'

In court, he admitted having owned a .32 pistol, but said that when he'd learnt that as a parolee it was a violation to own a firearm, he threw the gun in a river.

On 26 June 1981, the jury took just three-and-a-half hours to find him guilty on all counts. He was sentenced to life imprisonment plus 90 years. That December, he was given another 35 years when a jury in Benton County, Oregon, convicted him of sodomy and weapons charges tied to another attack in a restaurant toilet.

As it seemed unlikely that he would ever be released there was little point in pursuing further prosecutions. He admitted nothing. However, DNA evidence later linked him to the murders of Fix, Jarvis, Eckard, Altig, and Reitz.

An officer following the I-5 case listed other victims. Twenty-one-year-old Sylvia Durante had been strangled in Seattle and dumped beside the highway in December 1979. Three months later, 19-year-old Marsha Weatter and 18-year-old Kathy Allen had vanished while hitchhiking along I-5. Their corpses had been found in May, after the eruption of the Mount Saint Helens volcano nearby. At least four women had died around Huntington Beach, California, while Woodfield was sunning himself in the area. All were killed in his trademark style.

Interviewing him in connection with unsolved crimes in July 2005, cold-case supervisor Paul Weatheroy said: 'I remember that his hair was perfect, feathered and combed; he had a perfectly even tan, nails manicured. He was very charismatic, which makes sense because he would lure victims and get them to let their guard down.'

They found common ground when Woodfield learnt that Weatheroy's son was a high school football star in Portland who went on to play for the Air Force. 'He loved talking about sports,' said Weatheroy. 'His high school career, playing in college, his time with Green Bay....'

According to Ann Rule, Woodfield even kept in his wallet a carbon copy of the airline tickets the Packers sent him back in June 1974.

Jim Lawrence, another detective in Portland's cold case unit, was struck most by Woodfield's utter lack of accountability or remorse – even decades later and in the face of indisputable evidence.

'If you're talking about somebody moving toward some form of rehabilitation, they had to at some point acknowledge they are responsible for their own behaviours,' said Lawrence. 'That is not Randy Woodfield.'

Combing the files, he came to a report of Woodfield's father visiting him in jail.

'It was a really short meeting,' Lawrence said. 'When the dad walked out, he told the detectives, "He's not the son I know."'

And if he was paroled tomorrow? 'He would re-offend, there's no doubt about it,' said Lawrence. 'Even to this day, he is still a stone-cold killer.'

Jennifer Furio, who published *The Serial Killer Letters* in 1998, included a couple from Woodfield. In them he was still blaming a mysterious 'Larry Moore' for the murders.

'Read the police report first filed by Det. Kominek, lead "Dick" who hypnotized the victim-witness, who helped police draw the composite drawing of "I-5 Killer" suspect!! Go figure,' wrote Woodfield.

'Now ask yourself why they would fight my defense counsel, to keep [Larry Moore] out of my trial for murder. Because they KNOW they messed up, and arrest this mass-murderer 4-5 weeks after my arrest in the "I-5 Bandit" crime spree. Even the blood-type evidence doesn't match my type (B Neg.), so Judge throws state's blood evidence out of court! But my jury had a right to hear how the first blood test revealed (A/B) typing, and after my arrest, it changes to a plain (B) type. No "negative" enzyme can be detected. Maybe (Larry Moore's) blood type is (A/B)?

'The 1986 "Break-In" at D.A. offices, stinks of an "Inside" corruption case! Only my file is ransacked – so go figure Jenny. They only charged me because of a "Line-Up" identification by [Lisa Garcia]. But she never ONCE picked me out of color, close-up photos! Or did she describe me in any police report! Even the ambulance attendants testified for me, they state Ms. Garcia was slightly wounded, with scalp wound, but clear thinking to describe a shorter, sandy-haired fella matching the mass-murderer (Larry Moore).'

The closest Woodfield came to admitting what he had done was when he joined MySpace in 2006. In his profile, he wrote: 'I spend the remainder of my days in prison because I have committed a murder along with many other crimes. I once tried out for the Green Bay Packers. The only reason I didn't make it is because the skills I had to offer they didn't need at the time.'

RANDY STEVEN KRAFT

The Scorecard Killer

WHILE STILL AT LARGE, Randy Steven Kraft was initially known as the Southern California Strangler. Then as the death toll mounted, he became the Freeway Killer. However, there were two other contenders for the soubriquet. One was Patrick Kearney, also known as the Trash Bag Killer (see page 236), who started his murderous career in 1962 and continued until he was arrested in July 1977, claiming as many as 43 lives. The other was William Bonin, who killed more than 21 young men and boys between May 1979 and his arrest in June 1980. Meanwhile, Kraft continued killing until 14 May 1983.

At around 1.10 am that day, two California Highway Patrol officers noticed a Toyota Celica weaving down Interstate 5 in Orange County. Suspecting the driver was drunk, they pulled the car over. The driver was Kraft, who got out, dumping the contents of a beer bottle as he did so. Officer Michael Sterling noticed that Kraft's jeans were unbuttoned. He admitted that he had been drinking, but denied being drunk. A roadside sobriety test showed that was not the case.

The other patrolman, Sergeant Michael Howard, approached the vehicle and found a man slumped in the passenger seat. There were beer bottles at his feet. His body was cold and he was clearly dead. He had been bound, strangled and his pants had been pulled down. There were tranquilizers and various prescription drugs in the car. The dead man was 25-year-old US Marine Terry Lee Gambrel, who was stationed at the El Toro air base and who had ingested enough of the prescription tranquilizer Ativan, mixed with alcohol, to kill him. Human blood was also found. It was not Gambrel's. Pictures of naked young men in various pornographic poses were also discovered and, in the boot of the car, was a ring binder containing coded notes that, it was soon discovered, referred to Kraft's murder victims. It was his scorecard.

Searching the home Kraft shared with his gay partner Jeffrey Seelig, the police found various items of clothing in the garage that did not appear to belong to the couple. One jacket belonged to a murder victim from Michigan who had been killed in December 1982. The couch in the apartment matched one in the Polaroids found in Kraft's car – three of the naked men posed there had been found dead. Fibres from the sofa matched those on a corpse found in Anaheim in April 1978, and Kraft's fingerprints matched those found at a murder scene in December 1975.

Initially Kraft was charged with the murder of Terry Gambrel. When Kraft pleaded not guilty, he was immediately charged with four more murders. Another charge of a torture-slaying followed a week later.

SEND IN THE MARINES

From the age of 20, Kraft was openly gay, sharing an apartment with a male friend from college and visiting gay bars. In 1966, he was arrested for lewd conduct, after propositioning an undercover policeman in Huntington Beach, but he got off with a warning for a first offence.

The Vietnam war was under way and he briefly joined the US Air Force, though was quickly discharged ostensibly on medical grounds. Back on the gay scene, he told friends: 'There's a part of me that you will never know.' Fourteen years later they would discover what he meant. His sexual preference was for fit and healthy Marines. Otherwise, young boys would do.

In March 1970, Kraft picked up 13-year-old runaway Joseph Fancher on Huntingdon Beach. He took him home, plied him with booze,

SAN QUENTIN STATE PRISON

KRAFT, R.

E-38700

CONDEMNED   06/12/07

When they looked in the boot of Kraft's car, they found a ring binder containing coded notes referring to his victims. It was his scorecard.

marijuana and pills, and showed him pictures of men having sex. When Fancher was semi-conscious, Kraft stripped and sodomized him.

After Kraft went to work the following day, Fancher escaped barefoot. Patrons of a nearby bar called an ambulance. After having his stomach pumped, Fancher led the police back to Kraft's apartment, where they found his shoes, illegal drugs and photographs of Kraft having sex with various men. However, the search had been done without a warrant, so the matter went no further.

After enrolling at Long Beach State University, Kraft moved in with classmate Jeff Graves. Nevertheless, he continued cruising gay bars for sex with strangers – preferably Marines.

His first murder victim was thought to be 30-year-old Wayne Dukette, whose naked body was found dumped alongside the Ortega Highway on 5 October 1971. He had gone missing on 20 September and the body was so badly decomposed it was not possible to accurately determine the cause of death, though a high level of alcohol was noted. Dukette worked at a gay bar on nearby Sunset Beach named 'The Stable'. The first entry on Kraft's scorecard read 'Stable'.

On Christmas Eve 1972, 20-year-old Marine Edward Moore was seen leaving Camp Pendleton. Two days later his body was found beside the 405 Freeway at Seal Beach, apparently dumped from a moving vehicle. He had been bound, strangled and bludgeoned. There were bite marks on his genitals and one of his socks had been forced up his rectum.

Six weeks later, the naked body of an unidentified man was found beside the Terminal Island Freeway in the Wilmington district of Los Angeles. About 18 years old, the victim had been strangled a day or two before he was found. He had a brown sock stuffed into his anus. There was an entry on Kraft's scorecard saying simply 'Wilmington'.

Two months later, the body of 17-year-old Kevin Bailey was found beside a road in Huntington Beach. Though fully clothed, except for his shoes and socks, he had been sodomized and castrated.

The next victim, also unidentified, was dismembered and the body parts scattered along the coast from Sunset Beach to San Pedro. It showed signs of bondage. The hands were not found.

The body of another 20-year-old was found alongside 405 Freeway at Seal Beach on 30 July. He had disappeared bar-hopping two days before. He was fully clothed but barefoot. His body showed signs of torture. He had been hung upside down, beaten and strangled. There were bite marks on his stomach and penis and, again, one of his socks was found inside his anus.

Twenty-three-year-old art student Vincent Cruz Mestas was also found clothed and barefoot with a sock in his anus when his body was recovered from a ravine in the San Bernardino mountains 113 km (70 miles) inland on 29 December. His hands were missing and plastic sandwich bags covered the bloody stumps. An object the size of a pencil had been forced up his penis before he died.

On 1 June 1974, the naked body of 20-year-old Malcolm Eugene Little, an unemployed truck driver from Alabama, was found propped up against a mesquite tree alongside Highway 86. He had been castrated and a branch rammed 15 cm (6 in) up his rectum.

A branch 122 cm (4 ft) long and 75 mm (3 in) in diameter had been shoved up the anus of 19-year-old James Dale Reeves whose body, naked except for a bloody T-shirt, was found in Irvine on 29 November 1974. He had disappeared while out cruising on Thanksgiving Day.

The naked body of 18-year-old Marine Roger Dickerson was discovered in a dead-end street in Laguna Beach on 22 June. There were bite marks on his penis and left nipple. Last seen in a bar in San Clemente, he told friends that he got a ride to LA. He had been sodomized and strangled.

The body of 25-year-old Thomas Paxton Lee was found by oilfield workers in the harbour at Long Beach on 3 August, fully clothed. The waiter and sometime gay hustler had last been seen in Wilmington the previous night. He had been strangled. Twenty-three-year-old Gary Wayne Cordova was also found fully clothed except for his shoes and socks on 12 August. His body had been dumped down an embankment near Cabot Road and Oso Parkway in Laguna Hills. He had disappeared while hitchhiking. The cause of death was an overdose of Valium and alcohol. As Lee and Cordova's bodies did not show the killer's trademark mutilations, they were not attributed to him at first.

The body of 17-year-old John William Leras was found floating in the surf at Sunset Beach on 4 January 1975. A wooden stake had been rammed up his rectum. He had last been seen getting off the bus near Ripples Bar on his way to try out the new roller skates he had got for Christmas at the nearby rink. The police found two sets of footprints where his body seemed to have been carried from a car park to the water. He had been strangled.

Twenty-four-year-old Craig Victor Jonaites was found next to the Golden Sails Hotel-Bar on the Pacific Coast Highway near Loynes Drive in Long Beach, fully clothed except for shoes and socks. In fact, he was wearing two pairs of trousers, one over the other. The cause of death was strangulation.

EVENING UP THE SCORE

Clearly a serial killer was at work. A task force was set up and an FBI profiler was called in. But the murders continued. On 29 March 1975, the head of 19-year-old Keith Crotwell was found near the Long Beach Marina. He was last seen getting into a black and white Mustang. The owner was Randy Kraft. He was questioned and told police he had dropped the youth alive and well at an all-night café. The police wanted to charge him with murder, but the LA County prosecutors would not proceed due to lack of evidence.

After this, Kraft stopped killing for a while. Then, on 3 January 1976, the naked body of 22-year-old Mark Hall was found tied to a sapling at the east end of Santiago Canyon. He was last seen leaving a New Year's Eve party in San Juan Capistrano two days before. He had been sodomized. His legs had been slashed with a knife. His eyes, face, chest and genitals were burnt with a cigarette lighter. A cocktail swizzle stick had been jammed through his penis with such force that it ruptured the bladder. His genitals had then been cut off and stuffed into his rectum, along with dirt and leaves.

In the midst of this spree, Kraft left Jeff Graves and moved in with 19-year-old Jeff Seelig. He then began killing teenagers. The bodies of six of them were dumped in bin bags. But the arrest of Trash Bag Killer Patrick Kearney in 1977 muddied the waters. Kearney typically shot his victims and denied using torture on them.

With Kearney in jail, the murders continued. The body of 19-year-old Marine Scott Hughes was found beside the 91 Freeway in Orange County on 16 April 1978. His genitals had been mutilated. So were those of 23-year-old Roland Young, who was found dead in Irvine, less than eight hours after being released from jail.

The body of another Marine, 23-year-old Richard Keith, was found on the northbound lane of I-5 on 19 June. The body had been pushed from a moving car, so it was suspected that two killers were involved. The victim had been bound and tortured.

Twenty-one-year-old Michael Inderbeiten, a truck driver from Long Beach, was found on 18 November, just feet from where Edward Moore had been dumped six years earlier. His eyes had been burned with a cigarette lighter. He had been sodomized and castrated.

The bodies of more than a dozen victims were dumped along the highways of southern California in 1979. They had been bound, tortured, sodomized, castrated and strangled. More murders continued in 1980, 1981 and 1982. They all showed the trademarks of the same killer.

The police tried to match the victims to Kraft's coded scorecard. Forty-five corresponded, though they could find no match for known victims Eric Church and Terry Gambrel. There were 65 entries on the lists, making a death toll of 67, 22 of whom had not been recovered or identified. Kraft was found guilty of 16 murders, one count of sodomy and one of emasculation.

During the penalty hearings, the defence claimed that abnormalities in Kraft's brain meant he could not control his emotions and impulses, while the prosecution insisted: 'There is nothing wrong with Mr Kraft's mind other than that he likes killing for sexual satisfaction.'

Kraft was sentenced to death. As it was suspected that he had an accomplice, the police were preparing to question his lover Jeff Graves when he died of an AIDS-related illness in 1987. Dennis McDougal, author of *Angel of Darkness*, reported that small-time criminal Bob Jackson confessed to murdering two hitchhikers with Kraft, though the authorities could not substantiate the claims.

Kraft sued McDougal for $62 million, for unjustly portraying him as a 'sick, twisted man' and damaging his prospects for future employment. The California Supreme Court dismissed the lawsuit as frivolous in June 1994.

DERRICK TODD LEE

The Baton Rouge Serial Killer

IN 2004, DERRICK TODD Lee was convicted of two murders he had committed in 2002. However, his murderous spree may have been going on for a decade by that point. The police department in Zachary, East Baton Rouge County, Louisiana, believed that he was responsible for the murder of 41-year-old Connie Warner in 1992 and the disappearance of 28-year-old Randi Mebruer in 1998. At the time, these cases were overlooked because the suspect what thought to be white, while Lee was an African-American.

The first victim we can be certain of was Gina Wilson Green, a 41-year-old nurse and office manager for Home Infusion Network. A divorcée, she lived alone in Baton Rouge, near Louisiana State University. Her body was found in her apartment on 23 September 2001. She had been sexually assaulted. The cause of death was strangulation. Her purse was missing, along with her Nokia mobile phone. DNA linked Lee to her death.

Seven months later, there was another killing. On 31 May 2002, the body of 22-year-old Charlotte Murray Pace, a graduate student at Louisiana State, was found by her roommate at a townhouse on Sharlo Avenue in Baton Rouge. She had been sexually assaulted and stabbed, though she had put up a furious fight, enough to wound her attacker. Again, her mobile phone was missing.

Another strange coincidence linked the two killings. Charlotte had moved into the townhouse only two days before. Previously she

Derrick Todd Lee appears in Fulton County Superior Court for an extradition hearing, 28 May 2003, in Atlanta, Georgia.

had lived just three doors away from Gina Green. The killer had also taken the keys to Charlotte's BMW and a silver ring, along with a tan and brown Louis Vuitton wallet that contained her driver's licence. The killer left behind a footprint – that of a Rawlings brand trainer, size 10 or 11. Unfortunately, it was a brand widely found in discount stores.

Then on 12 July 2002, Pam Kinamore went missing. She was an antiques dealer who ran her own business, Comforts and Joys, in Denham Springs, a few miles east of Baton Rouge. It was a Friday evening and she shut up shop as usual before driving home to 8338 Briarwood Place in Baton Rouge itself. When her husband arrived home later, his wife's car was there but she was nowhere to be seen. Later, when she did not show up, he phoned the police and reported her missing.

Four days later, a team of surveyors working in a boggy area of woodland under the Whisky Bay Bridge in Iberville Parish between Baton Rouge and Lafayette saw something at the water's edge. It was the naked body of a dead woman. She was identified as Pam Kinamore. The cause of death was a knife wound to the neck and she had been sexually assaulted. A silver toe ring that she wore was missing. The police quickly tied her killing to those of Gina Green and Charlotte Pace – and another case.

Two days after Pam Kinamore had gone missing, a 28-year-old Mississippian woman was raped by a man who had forced her into a white pickup on Interstate 10 that runs westwards from Baton Rouge to Lafayette. After the assault, he had let her go and she gave the police a good enough description of her attacker for them to put together a composite.

Then, a week after Kinamore's body had been found, a woman came forward claiming that she had seen a woman answering Kinamore's description slumped in the passenger seat of a white pickup truck the night she had gone missing. She appeared to be sleeping or was, perhaps, dead. The truck had been speeding westwards down Interstate

10 at around 3 am. It had turned off at the Whisky Bay exit near where Pam Kinamore's body was found. The driver was, she said, a white male.

PIECING TOGETHER A PROFILE

The police now had a good description of the vehicle. They were looking for a white General Motors, or possibly a Chevrolet, pickup truck, thought to be a 1996–97 single cab model. The licence plate was thought to contain JT341, though it was not known which state had issued it. A witness also said she had seen the shape of a fish on the rear off-side of the pickup.

In August 2002, a multi-agency murder task force was formed, comprising 40 officers from local police departments, sheriffs' offices, the Louisiana State Police and the FBI. Already they had DNA evidence linking the murders of Gina Green and Charlotte Pace. Later the Louisiana State Crime Lab managed to show that Kinamore had been killed by the same man. Now certain that they had a serial killer on the loose, the police began combing through unsolved homicides from the last ten years. They also had fresh cases to add to the list.

On 21 November 2002, 23-year-old Trineisha Dene Colomb disappeared. At around 1.30 pm her black 1994 Mazda MX3 was found on Robbie Road in the small town of Grand Coteau, 80 km (50 miles) west of Baton Rouge. The keys were still in the ignition, but Colomb was nowhere to be seen. Her naked body was found by a rabbit hunter in a wood 48 km (30 miles) away three days later. Colomb had been a US Marine and fought back while being bludgeoned to death. DNA evidence linked Colomb's killer with the Green, Pace and Kinamore murders.

Another footprint was found, again of a man's athletic shoe in size 10 or 11. This one was the latest model of an Adidas-style basketball shoe. Again, it was on sale widely in the area. Some of the victim's possessions were missing, including a ring with the world 'Love' inscribed on it.

There were some unique features, though. This was the first time the killer had struck outside Baton Rouge itself and Colomb was thought to be the Baton Rouge serial killer's first known black victim.

On the day Colomb went missing, a white pickup truck was seen in the same wooded area where her body was found. The driver was described as around 35 years old and white, and investigators put together a new composite which was later released as a 'person of interest'.

The task force actively solicited help from the public. In November 2002, DNA samples were taken from 600 volunteers using mouth swabs. Samples were taken from a further 100 potential suspects the following month.

The police then took the unusual step of issuing a detailed profile of the man they sought. He was probably in a low-paid occupation that required physical strength, such as construction. He had shown himself strong enough to subdue a US Marine and carry the dead body of Pam Kinamore over a boggy terrain.

The killer, the profiler said, was insecure around women, particularly women who displayed any sort of sophistication. Most women would have thought him awkward, but dismissed him as harmless. There was evidence he had stalked his victims before attacking them. And though the killer was sometimes impulsive, the murders seemed to have been planned.

The profiler also believed that the murderer would be preoccupied with news of the killings. If irritated by the coverage, it was thought he might give himself away. So, in an attempt to provoke him, the task force used electronic billboards to keep the public up to date with the investigation. However, the tactic failed. After 18 months they seemed no closer to catching the killer.

The task force then drew flak from Dr Robert Keppel, the noted criminologist who had been involved in the investigations of the

Green River Killer and Ted Bundy. He criticized the use of the media. Releasing details of the killer's shoe prints might cause him to destroy the identifying footwear, making it more difficult to prove the case if he was caught. And revealing the DNA links between the victims would warn the killer to take more care about leaving behind genetic evidence in future crimes. Keppel was no fan of psychological profiling either. Instead, the task force should comb its files which probably contained the killer's name already, overlooked in the deluge of information that was flooding in because of the media campaign.

Early in 2003, the Baton Rouge serial killer struck again. The next victim was Carrie Lynn Yoder, a 26-year-old postgraduate student at Louisiana State. She lived alone at 4250 Dodson Avenue not far from Charlotte Pace and Gina Green. On 3 March, she told Lee Stanton, her boyfriend of three years, that she was going to the Winn Dixie grocery store on Burbank Drive. They arranged to talk again later that night or the following day. When she did not call he began to worry.

On 4 March, he drove by her house and noted that the lights were on and her car was outside, but he left it at that. The next day, when he still had not heard from her, he went back to the house. The back door was open and he went in. Her keys, purse and mobile phone were on the worktop. Everything else seemed to be in order, except for a wall-mounted key rack near the front door. It was hanging by one screw as if it had been dislodged by some considerable force. To Stanton, it looked like there had been a struggle in that area and he called the police.

Searching the house, they found a well-stocked fridge and cupboards, indicating that Carrie Yoder had returned from the store before she went missing. Questionnaires were handed out at the Winn Dixie. Meanwhile, helicopters searched the area.

Ten days after she had gone missing, an angler found Carrie Yoder's body in the Atchafalaya River near the Whisky Bay Bridge – not far from where Pam Kinamore's body had been dumped eight months before. She had been badly beaten and she had put up a fierce fight before she had been strangled. DNA evidence showed that Carrie Yoder was the fifth victim of the Baton Rouge serial killer.

On 17 March the family and friends of the victims staged a demonstration on the steps of the Louisiana state capitol in Baton Rouge, demanding that something be done. The task force's response was to tell the public that they should ignore the composites previously circulated. They were now looking for a man of any race or description. Nor should they only be on the lookout for white pickups. The killer might be using a vehicle of any type as no white truck had been spotted in connection with Carrie Yoder's murder.

A week later, Melinda McGhee, a 31-year-old mother of two, disappeared from her home in Atmore, Alabama. She worked as a nurse in a nearby nursing home. She called her mother and her husband from there sometime before 8.30 am on the morning of her disappearance. In her home, there were signs of a struggle, but no evidence of murder. Although Melinda McGhee's home was some 354 km (220 miles) from Baton Rouge, it was easy to get to on the Interstate and there were striking similarities between McGhee's disappearance and those of Kinamore and Yoder. However, no body was found.

Another name was added to the list of victims on 8 April. This was not a new case, but one that had been overlooked before. On 10 February 2002, the naked body of Lillian Robinson, a 52-year-old prostitute from St Martin Parish between Lafayette and Baton Rouge, had been found in the Atchafalaya River, near Whisky Bay Bridge. She had gone missing the previous month.

Another woman had possibly fallen victim to the Baton Rouge serial killer in May 2002, when the car of Christine Moore, a 23-year-old student at Louisiana State, was found abandoned near River Road in Baton Rouge. She had left home to go jogging at a park, but never returned. Her body was found on a dirt road in Iberville Parish in June. Like Trineisha Colomb she had been bludgeoned to death. Despite its similarities to the other killings, her death was not formally attributed to the Baton Rouge serial killer.

SCIENCE COMES TO THE RESCUE

The investigation then took a surprising turn on 23 May 2003, when Fox News reported that the task force was looking into three incidents in which a young black man attacked women in St Martin Parish, though none of them was killed. A composite was produced showing a light-skinned African-American male who said his name was Anthony and, initially, tried to charm his victims. Until then, it was assumed that the Baton Rouge serial killer was white.

On 5 May DNA swabs were taken from a man who resembled the composite and were sent to the crime labs for analysis. They matched the DNA taken from the body of Carrie Yoder and linked the suspect to three more victims of the Baton Rouge serial killer.

The DNA belonged to 34-year-old Derrick Todd Lee, who lived in St Francisville in West Feliciana Parish, 32 km (20 miles) north of Baton Rouge. He had given the sample voluntarily nearly three weeks earlier, but later that same day his wife Jacqueline Denise Lee took their two children out of school, saying the family was moving to Los Angeles. Packing up their belongings, they in fact fled to Chicago, while Derrick Todd Lee moved on to Atlanta.

On 26 May an arrest warrant was issued for Lee. The following day he was apprehended in a tyre store in Atlanta. For a week he had been living in the Lakewood Motor Lodge, where other residents found him to be a 'very nice man'. He had even charmed a number of women there, inviting them back to his room for a glass of cognac. Lee waived extradition proceedings and was flown back to Louisiana voluntarily the next day. Initially, he was charged with the murder of Carrie Yoder.

However, by early June he was also accused of the rape and murder of Gina Green, Charlotte Pace, Pam Kinamore and Trineisha Colomb.

What confounded the authorities was that Lee did not fit the typical profile of a serial killer. Lee was black, with a wife and two children and was outgoing and charming to everyone he met, not a solitary middle-aged white male who was awkward, introverted and a loner. Nor did Lee fit the profile drawn up specifically for this case.

He did, however, have a criminal record that stretched back to 1984 when, at the age of 15, he was caught peeping into the window of a woman's home in St Francisville.

A string of arrests for peeping, stalking, as well as illegal entry, burglary, assault and resisting arrest followed. In January 2000, he had been accused of attempted murder after severely kicking his girlfriend Consandra Green after an argument over Lee's advances towards another woman in a bar. While fleeing the police, he tried to run over the sheriff's deputy and got two years. After being released the following year, he was arrested for wife-beating, but the charges were dropped. It was said that his wife 'lived in denial of her husband's transgressions, which include stalking, peeping into windows and infidelity'. At one point, she let him move a mistress into the family home.

The police were particularly eager to trace Lee's wife Jacqueline. She was found by the FBI with the couple's two children in Chicago in June. The police had received an anonymous tip-off that more bodies had been buried under a concrete slab at the couple's home and needed her consent to dig there.

They also set about excavating the driveway at the former home of Lee's girlfriend Consandra Green as Lee had been seen pouring concrete there in the middle of the night only a couple of days after Randi Mebruer had disappeared from her home in Zachary in 1998. A woman's bracelet was found, but the search for human remains drew a blank at both sites. The police in Bolton, Mississippi, also tried to tie

Lee to the slayings of four women found near a truck stop as he had once been a truck driver.

Investigators were still puzzled by the white pickup seen in the early murders. They impounded a truck from Consandra Green's uncle, said to have been sold to him by Lee, but no connection was established with the murders. Besides, the driver of the pickup was said to have been white.

A QUESTION OF DEGREES

On 24 September 2003, Lee was formally indicted for the first-degree murder of Trineisha Dene Colomb of Lafayette, Louisiana. However, the district attorney decided not to take that case to trial. Meanwhile, DNA evidence failed to link Lee to the murder of Connie Warner.

The following Wednesday, he was charged with the attempted rape and murder of Diane Alexander, a nurse in Breaux Bridge outside Lafayette. She claimed that Lee had beaten her and tried to rape and strangle her in her trailer in 2002 – and would have succeeded if her son had not come home and scared him off. Lee was also charged with the murder of 21-year-old Geralyn DeSoto, who was found beaten and stabbed in her mobile home at Addis, across the Mississippi from Baton Rouge, on 12 January 2002 – the day she registered as a graduate student at Louisiana State. This was a second-degree murder charge because the prosecution felt it could not prove an underlying felony, such as forced entry or rape, which was needed for the charge of first-degree murder in Louisiana.

Lee was found guilty of the second-degree murder of Geralyn DeSoto on 10 August 2004. The verdict brought a mandatory life sentence. On 12 October, Lee was found guilty of the first-degree murder of Charlotte Murray Pace after the prosecution was allowed to introduce evidence from other suspected Baton Rouge serial killer cases to prove a pattern. He was sentenced to death by lethal injection. As he was taken from the courtroom he shouted: 'God don't sleep.' Then he cried: 'They don't want to tell them about the DNA they took eight times.'

On 16 January 2008, the state Supreme Court upheld the murder conviction and death sentence. Lee was sent to death row at the Louisiana State Penitentiary in Angola, but died of heart disease in hospital on 21 January 2016.

MAURY TRAVIS

The Streetwalker Strangler

IN 2001 AND 2002, a serial killer was on the loose in St Louis. The bodies of streetwalking crackheads were being dumped around the city. They showed signs of torture. Because the victims were drug addicts, prostitutes and black, Bill Smith of the *St Louis Post-Despatch* figured that the investigation was not making progress because the victims were considered 'throw-away people' and he was determined to do something about it.

Smith decided to concentrate on one of the cases – that of 36-year-old Teresa Wilson. Like several of the victims, she worked from a strip on Broadway just north of St Louis where there were plenty of crack houses, leaving her daughter Chastity on a bench while she turned tricks in clients' cars. One night she did not come back. On 15 May 2001, her decomposed body was found in undergrowth in West Alton, just north of the city, at a site where rubbish and the bodies of two other women were dumped.

After the story was published on 18 May, Smith received a letter which read: 'Dear Bill, nice sob story about Teresa Wilson. Write one about greenwade write a good one and I'll tell you where many others are to prove im real here's directions to number seventeen search in a fifty yard radius from the x put the story in the Sunday paper like last.' The body of 34-year-old Alysa Greenwade had been found on 1 April, 8 km (5 miles) away in Washington Park.

Accompanying the letter was a map of West Alton. Smith called the police, who found the body of an unidentified woman at the point marked by hand on the map. They noticed that the map had been downloaded from the internet. Detectives trawled websites that carried maps of the area and discovered that the one the killer had sent came from Expedia.com.

The FBI then subpoenaed the records of the maps of West Alton held by Microsoft, who said just one computer had downloaded such a map. They had no name, but its Internet Protocol address was 65.227.106.78. Armed with the IP address, the FBI turned to WorldCom Inc., the company that provided local telephone numbers to connect internet services to dial-up customers. WorldCom assigns a temporary IP address for each internet session to each customer using dial-up services. On the evening of 20 May, the user had been MSN/maurytravis. Microsoft then identified the customer as Maury Troy Travis of Ferguson, Missouri, a suburb of St Louis.

Travis – the man the newspapers had been calling the Streetwalker Strangler – was the first serial killer tracked down via the internet. The police knocked on his door early in the morning of 7 June. He was still sleeping.

'It's seven o'clock in the morning,' said Travis, answering the door in his underwear. 'Why are you here so early?'

'You know why we're here,' they told him.

After Travis had dressed, the police sat him down in the lounge and Sergeant Tim Sachs, a 22-year veteran of the St Louis Police Department, and an FBI profiler and expert on serial killers, began questioning him.

'Where did you grow up?' they asked him.

'Where did *you* grow up?' he responded.

'What did you do as a child?' they asked.

'Nothing. Went to school. What did you do?' he said.

This verbal fencing went on for two hours.

'He kept trying to redirect everything, every question,' said Sachs. 'He wanted to be in control.'

Travis never once asked police why they had come or why they were sitting in his house, questioning him. He never admitted anything, but he never denied anything either. Only one thing interested him – how they had been able to find him.

'He wanted to know what led us here, how we knew that he was the guy,' Sachs said.

Finally, investigators told him about the map he had downloaded from the internet. He 'had a problem', they told him. Travis cursed the computer.

'Damned internet,' he said.

Then the police took him to police headquarters downtown.

MANNERS MAKETH THE MAN

Maury Travis was a 36-year-old waiter. Born in St Louis, he moved with his family into a simple ranch house in Ferguson when he was ten. Three years later, his parents divorced. His mother remarried, but divorced again in 1993.

A neighbour described Maury as a quiet, respectful boy, a pleasant child with a soft heart who sometimes mowed her lawn without being asked and showed her how to use an electric hedge trimmer.

'I don't believe he could kill a fly,' she said.

At school he was withdrawn and passed almost unnoticed. Only his English teacher at high school still remembered him at the time of his arrest. She said he was incredibly quiet for a teenager.

'Even the quiet ones can be noisy sometimes,' she said, 'but not him.' After graduating, he spent two years in the US Army Reserve, working as a medical and dental assistant. Then he took a number of jobs with trucking companies in the area and volunteered at a local nursing home.

In 1987, Travis, then 22, enrolled at Morris Brown College in Atlanta, a school affiliated with the African Methodist Episcopal Church. Around that time, he became addicted to cocaine. Soon he had a $300-a-day habit. In March 1988, he was arrested after sticking up five shoe stores. In court, he pleaded guilty, saying that he had used a toy gun and was so strung out he could barely remember the offences. The judge received letters of support, including one from a Congressman, saying that his crime spree was an aberration caused by his drug habit.

Travis assured the judge he had gone through a drug rehabilitation programme and was clean.

'I got all that stuff out of my system,' he said. He was rehabilitated.

Nevertheless, he was sentenced to 15 years. Soon he was suicidal. He wrote to the judge, saying: 'The conditions here are excruciatingly tormenting to say the least. Staying in my cell and crying myself to sleep most every night will not help, but it's so very hard to believe this has happened to me.'

He complained of the cramped living conditions, the poor food, the proliferation of drugs and homosexual rape – though he did not claim that he had been raped himself. Paroled after five years, he found himself back in jail two more times for drug-related offences. Nevertheless, a neighbour, the Reverend Linda Harrison, found him polite and considerate.

Working as a waiter in the Mayfair Hotel in downtown St Louis, co-worker Dave Wucher remembered Travis counselling him on the dangers of drugs and talking about his black 2000 Mitsubishi Eclipse, which was his pride and joy. He also told Wucher about a friend whose car was stolen and later found burning in East St Louis.

'Maury told me that East St Louis was a good place to dump things because there's not many police around,' Wucher said. The bodies of at least four of Travis' victims were found in East St Louis.

Wucher's girlfriend Julie Kroenig was working as an intern for KDNL (Channel 30) news in July 2000 when Travis asked if her TV station had done a story on the prostitutes getting killed.

'He said he had friends who knew about bodies getting dumped,' Kroenig said. Travis had specifically mentioned that a serial killer was responsible. This was three months before the police said publicly in a *Post-Dispatch* story that a serial killer was preying on local prostitutes.

A CELLAR FULL OF SECRETS

Travis was a little more helpful when he got downtown. Sachs asked him about girlfriends. He said he dated. Indeed, he had been engaged, but his fiancée had moved out in March 2001. This was shortly before the killings started. He also admitted using prostitutes.

Had he been abused as a child, Sachs asked him.

'No,' Travis said. 'How about you?'

Asked whether the crimes he was suspected of were a product of nature or nurture, he said he had been born like this. He'd been this way since he could remember.

While he was being questioned, the police were searching Travis' house. They found the basement had been converted into a makeshift torture chamber. Blood was soaked into the carpet. The walls had been repeatedly repainted to cover the stains. In a filing cabinet, they found bondage equipment and restraints covered in blood. There was a stun gun – some of the bodies had been found with burn marks. Travis also kept a scrapbook of press cuttings about the murders he was suspected of.

The police also found numerous videotapes showing him giving the prostitutes crack cocaine to smoke, then having consensual sex with them. He apparently let some of the women leave at that point. Some of the videos were more sinister. A tape labelled *Your Wedding Day* began with a shot of a woman sitting on the bed. It was captioned: 'Another crackhead ho.'

He would get victims to dance in white clothes, wearing glasses with blacked out lenses. Then he would harangue them either in the bedroom or after he had shackled them naked to a post.

In one scene with an unidentified victim, he taunted: 'You want to say something to your kids?' She answered: 'I'm sorry.'

'Who's raising your kids?' he asked.

'Me, my mom and dad.'

'You ain't raising shit, bitch,' he said. 'You over here on your back smoking crack. You ain't going home tomorrow. I'm keeping you about a week. Is that all right?'

He forced one victim to say: 'You are the master. It pleases me to serve you.'

'Say it clearer!' he yelled.

When another victim tried to remove the duct tape covering her eyes Travis told her: 'You don't need to see shit. Lay down on your back. Shut your eyes.'

Cries of agony came from one woman as he ordered her to sit still!

Excerpts released by the police did not include actual torture, except in one case where Travis was shown wrapping a belt around a woman's neck and snapping it tight, choking her until her body went limp. Travis then left the woman's naked body face down on the floor saying, 'This is first kill. Number One. First kill was 19 years old. Name – I don't know. I don't give a f***.'

Police who viewed the entire tape said it showed Travis raping the women and penetrating them with foreign objects. The scenes on the tape were so disturbing that police chief Joe Mokwa ordered psychological counselling for the officers who viewed them. 'They'll give you nightmares,' he told ABC News' *Primetime*.

'You know what we found in your basement?' Sachs asked Travis.

'Yeah, I knew you'd find it,' he replied.

He dropped his head and said: 'I'm toast.'

TAKING THE EASY WAY OUT

Initially Maury Troy Travis was charged with the kidnapping, torturing and killing of Alysa Greenwade and Betty James. Tyre impressions found next to Greenwade's body and on James' leg appeared consistent with the tyres on Travis' 1992 Chevrolet Cavalier and 2000 Mitsubishi Eclipse, the authorities said. Federal court documents showed that evidence linked him to seven murders in all and that he would face the death penalty.

But Travis was adamant.

'I am not going back to prison,' he told his interrogators. 'I am not going back.'

He was right. Three days after his arrest he managed to commit suicide, even though he was on suicide watch with a guard stationed outside his cell door. During a one-hour shower break when the guard did not have a clear view of all of his cell, Travis managed to hang himself in the back corner by threading a strip of braided sheet though a ventilator grille and fashioning a noose. He pulled a pillowcase over his head then, somehow, tied his hands behind his back. He climbed on to the commode, slipped the noose over his head and jumped off.

His suicide note was addressed to his mother. It read:

Dear Mom,

I am sorry for the pain this has caused you and the family. My death seems to be the only way out and a fast end to all the publicity. You were the best mother a man can have. But I've been sick for a long time (sick in the head) since I was about 14. I don't know why. I was just sick. I've never felt normal or happy at any time in my life. I think about the life I lead and what's ahead of me. This seams the best solution for all involved because I won't spend the rest of my life locked up or worse let them kill me with a needle....

The police only managed to identify 12 victims, though Travis had boasted of killing 17.

'Who are these other women and where are they?' said Mokwa. 'There's some families out here that have a lost loved one, and they'll always be uncertain of what happened to them.'

DONALD HARVEY

The Angel of Death

CLAIMING SOME 87 VICTIMS, Donald Harvey is possibly America's most prolific serial killer. Working as a hospital orderly, he murdered patients in what he claimed were mercy killings. However, he also let his murderous ways spill out into his personal life.

On the surface there was little clue in his early life that Harvey would turn out a serial killer. His mother said that he had 'always been a good boy' and the principal of his elementary school said: 'He was always clean and well dressed with his hair trimmed. He was a happy child, very sociable and well-liked by the other children. He was a handsome boy with big brown eyes and dark curly hair... he always had a smile for me. There was never any indication of any abnormality.'

However, it appears that his parents had an abusive relationship. His father dropped him when he was just six months old, before the soft spot had closed. He suffered another head injury at the age of five when he fell off the running board of a truck. Although he did not lose consciousness, there was a cut 10–13 cm (4–5 in) long on the back of his head.

From the age of four he was sexually abused by his Uncle Wayne. A neighbour also sexually abused him, but Harvey did not mind this as the old man gave him money.

At high school, his classmates saw him as a teachers' pet who would rather have his nose stuck in a book than play sports. He did well academically, initially. But learning came too easily. He grew bored and dropped out. He had his first consensual sexual encounter when he was 16. The following year he began an on-off sexual relationship with James Peluso that lasted for 15 years.

With little direction in life, Harvey left Booneville, Kentucky, and moved to Cincinnati, where he got a job in a factory. In 1970, he was laid off. His mother asked him to visit his ailing grandfather who was in Marymount Hospital in London, Kentucky. Spending time there, he got to know the staff.

One of them asked Harvey if he wanted a job as an orderly. Unemployed at the time, he jumped at the chance. Though he had no medical training, his duties included passing out medication, inserting catheters and changing bedpans. The job meant he spent time alone with patients. Around that period, he claimed he was raped by his roommate.

AN ANGRY YOUNG MAN

While Harvey made out that he was a mercy killer, his first murder was motivated by anger. He later told Dan Horn of the *Cincinnati Post* that when he went to check on 88-year-old stroke victim Logan Evans in his private room, the patient rubbed faeces in his face. Harvey lost control.

'The next thing I knew, I'd smothered him,' he said. 'It was like it was the last straw. I just lost it. I went in to help the man and he wants to rub that in my face.'

Harvey put a sheet of blue plastic and a pillow over the old man's face and listened to his heartbeat with a stethoscope until he was dead. He disposed of the plastic and cleaned him up, dressing Evans in a fresh hospital gown. Then he had a shower before notifying the nurse on duty of Evans' death. Harvey had no fear of getting caught.

'No one ever questioned it,' he said.

Donald Harvey suffered a couple of serious head injuries when he was young. He was also sexually abused by his Uncle Wayne.

The following day he said he accidentally killed 69-year-old James Tyree when he used the wrong-sized catheter on him. When Tyree yelled at him to take it out, Harvey silenced him with the heel of his hand. Tyree then vomited blood and died.

Three weeks later came the first of what could be considered mercy killings. Forty-two-year-old Elizabeth Wyatt told him she wanted to die, so he turned down her oxygen supply. Four hours later, a nurse found her dead.

The following month, he killed 43-year-old Eugene McQueen by turning him on his stomach when he knew he wasn't supposed to. McQueen drowned in his own fluids. Harvey told the nurse merely that McQueen looked bad and she told him to continue with his duties. Consequently, Harvey gave McQueen a bath even though he was already dead. For as long as he worked at Marymount, the staff teased Harvey for bathing a dead man.

He accidently killed 82-year-old Harvey Williams when a gas tank proved faulty. But the next death at his hands was premeditated murder. Eighty-one-year-old Ben Gilbert knocked him out with a bedpan and poured its contents over him, saying that he thought Harvey was a burglar. Harvey retaliated by catheterizing Gilbert with a female-sized 20-gauge catheter instead of the smaller 18-gauge used for men. He then straightened out a coat hanger and shoved the wire through the catheter, puncturing Gilbert's bladder and bowel. Gilbert went into shock and fell into a coma. Harvey disposed of the wire and replaced the 20-gauge catheter with an 18-gauge. Ben Gilbert died four days later.

Harvey began a seven-month relationship with Vernon Midden, a married man who had children. He was an undertaker who taught Harvey the tricks of the trade and introduced him to the occult. When the relationship went sour the following January, Harvey fantasized about embalming him alive.

KILLING AS AN ACT OF KINDNESS?

Maude Nichols had been so neglected that her bedsores crawled with maggots. When she arrived at Marymount, Harvey fixed her up with a faulty oxygen tank. He simply neglected to turn on the oxygen for 58-year-old William Bowling, who had difficulty breathing and subsequently died of a heart attack.

A faulty oxygen tank also did for 63-year-old Viola Reed Wyan after his attempt to smother her was interrupted. She had leukaemia and Harvey complained that she smelt bad. Ninety-one-year-old Margaret Harrison was despatched with an overdose of Demerol, morphine and codeine that was intended for another patient.

Harvey decided that 80-year-old Sam Carroll had suffered enough and he was given a faulty oxygen tank. Maggie Rawlins was smothered with a plastic bag. Both 62-year-old Silas Butner and 68-year-old John V. Combs were killed with faulty oxygen tanks after attempts to smother them had failed. Ninety-year-old Milton Bryant Sasser was killed with an overdose of morphine which Harvey had stolen from the nurse's station. Harvey tried to dispose of the syringe by flushing it down the lavatory, where it was found by a maintenance man. Harvey left Marymount Hospital soon after. He was still only 18.

Harvey then had his first heterosexual encounter. He got drunk with the daughter of the family he was staying with and they ended up naked. Nine months later she had a child, naming Harvey as the father, though he rejected any responsibility.

Depressed, Harvey tried to kill himself by setting fire to the bathroom of an empty apartment. He was arrested and fined $50. Then he was arrested on suspicion of burglary, though the police really wanted to question him about his involvement with the occult. During the interview, he admitted killing 15 people at Marymount Hospital, but they did not believe him.

He briefly enlisted in the US Air Force, but was discharged after trying to commit suicide. A further suicide attempt landed him in a Veterans' Administration Hospital after his parents would not take him in.

In 1972, he started work at the Cardinal Hill Convalescent Hospital in Lexington, Kentucky. It is not thought he killed anyone there. For ten months he lived with Russell Addison. This was followed by a five-year relationship with Ken Estes.

In September 1975, he became a nursing assistant at the VA Hospital in Lexington. He tampered with the oxygen supply for Joseph Harris, possibly resulting in his death. Harvey also claimed he had a hand in the deaths of James Twitty, James Ritter, Harry Rhodes and Sterling Moore.

To be initiated into the local occult group, Harvey had to hook up with a woman, so they could then swap partners with another couple. This resulted in the conception of another child, though Harvey denied any responsibility once again. He also acquired a spirit guide named Duncan, a doctor during his lifetime, who now directed him to kill from beyond the grave.

POISONOUS RELATIONSHIP

In 1980, Harvey began dating Doug Hill. When they fell out, Harvey attempted to poison him by putting arsenic in his ice cream. In August, he moved in with Carl Hoeweler. When he found Carl was fooling around with other men, he put small doses of arsenic in his food to prevent him going out. Fearing that Carl's 'fag hag' friend Diane Alexander was trying to split them up, he gave her hepatitis-B serum stolen from the hospital. He also tried unsuccessfully to infect her with AIDS.

His 63-year-old neighbour Helen Metzger was also considered a threat and murdered with arsenic in her food, though Harvey contended he did not mean to give her a lethal dose. Her family got sick from leftovers served at the funeral. Carl's 82-year-old father Henry was also despatched by arsenic. Carl's brother-in-law Howard Vetter was killed accidentally, Harvey claimed, when he left wood alcohol in a vodka bottle. Harvey also murdered another neighbour, Edward Wilson, who he thought was a threat to his relationship with Carl Hoeweler. Wilson was despatched with arsenic in his Pepto-Bismol bottle.

Harvey killed Hiram Profitt accidentally, giving him the wrong dose of heparin. Former boyfriend James Peluso, then 65, asked Harvey to help him out if ever he could not take care of himself. Harvey put arsenic in his daiquiri.

After he joined the neo-Nazi National Socialist Party, Harvey was fired from the VA Hospital in 1985 for carrying a gun in his gym bag. Body parts which he intended to use in occult practices were also found. The following year, he started a new job at Daniel Drake Memorial Hospital in Cincinnati.

After six weeks, he smothered 65-year-old Nathan J. Watson with a bin bag after several thwarted attempts. Watson was semi-comatose and was fed through a gastric tube and Harvey said he didn't think anyone should live that way. He also believed Watson to have been a rapist.

Four days later, 64-year-old Leon Nelson was despatched the same way. A week after that 81-year-old Virgil Weddle was killed with rat poison. Cookies stolen from him were used in rites for Duncan. Rat poison was also used to kill Lawrence Berndsen the next day.

Harvey put cyanide in 65-year-old Doris Nally's apple juice. Sixty-three-year-old Edward Schreibesis got arsenic in his soup, though arsenic failed to kill Willie Johnson. Eighty-year-old Robert Crockett succumbed to cyanide in his IV. Sixty-one-year-old Donald Barney had cyanide injected in his buttocks, while 65-year-old James T. Wood was given cyanide in his gastric tube. Eighty-five-year-old Ernst C. Frey got arsenic the same way.

Eighty-five-year-old Milton Canter got cyanide in a nasal tube. Seventy-four-year-old Roger Evans ingested it in his gastric tube. Sixty-four-year-old Clayborn Kendrick got it the same way. More cyanide was injected into his testes.

Cyanide was given to 86-year-old Albert Buehlmann in a cup of water and to 85-year-old William Collins in orange juice. Seventy-eight-year-old Henry Cody had it fed through his gastric tube.

Following his break-up with Carl, Harvey was treated for depression and tried to kill himself by driving off a mountain road, injuring his head. Sixty-five-year-old Mose Thompson and 72-year-old Odas Day were despatched with solutions of cyanide, while 67-year-old Cleo Fish got it in her cranberry juice. Two other patients were given arsenic but survived, while 47-year-old Leo Parker succumbed to cyanide in his feed bag.

Eighty-year-old Margaret Kuckro got it in her orange juice, as did 76-year-old Stella Lemon. Sixty-eight-year-old Joseph M. Pike and 82-year-old Hilda Leitz were despatched with the adhesive remover Detachol. Forty-four-year-old John W. Powell was killed with cyanide in his gastric feeding tube. An autopsy was performed and the pathologist smelt bitter almonds – the characteristic aroma of cyanide. Three laboratories confirmed its presence and the Cincinnati Police Department was notified.

Harvey came under suspicion because of his sacking from the VA Hospital. He called in sick the day that staff were given polygraph tests. When questioned, he admitted killing Powell, saying he felt sorry for him and denied killing anyone else.

Pat Minarcin, then an anchor at WCPO-TV in Cincinnati, figured that if he had killed once he might have done it on other occasions. Digging into Harvey's past, he managed to link him to 24 murders, filling a half-hour special report.

Court-appointed defence attorney Bill Whalen cut a plea bargain. If the death penalty was taken off the table, he said, Harvey would confess to all the murders. In August 1987 in Ohio, Donald Harvey pleaded guilty to 24 counts of murder and was sentenced to three concurrent terms of life. That November in Kentucky he pleaded guilty to another nine murders, giving him another life sentence plus 20 years. In the end, the self-styled Angel of Death pleaded guilty to 37 murders, though he admitted many more.

Incarcerated in Toledo Correctional Institution, he was found badly battered in his cell on 28 March 2017 and died two days later. Fellow inmate James Elliott was charged with his murder.

SURINDER KOLI

The Butcher of Noida

IN 2005 AND 2006, children began going missing in the village of Nithari on the outskirts of Noida, an industrial township in Uttar Pradesh near Delhi. The fathers of two of the missing girls, aged ten and eight, heard rumours that the children's remains were scattered around a compound by a massive water tank behind house number D-5. The property belonged to wealthy businessman Moninder Singh Pandher, but they suspected his servant Surinder Koli was responsible.

The two men went to the police, who turned a deaf ear. So, they sought the help of the former president of the local Residents Welfare Association. On 26 December 2006, they began to clean out a blocked drain where, after half an hour, they found a decomposed hand. Koli was arrested. He then confessed to killing six children after sexually assaulting them, along with a 20-year-old woman known as 'Payal'. She was a call girl who visited Pandher, but her mobile phone was in the possession of a rickshaw driver who said that Koli had sold it to him.

The police soon unearthed the dismembered parts of 17 bodies in front of and behind Pandher's residence. Koli identified ten of the skeletons, while the families identified another five from the belongings unearthed at the scene.

'The bodies were kept in bags and buried near a drain behind the house. We have also recovered some clothes of children,' said Jagmohan

Yadav, inspector general of police. 'We have also found weapons while searching the house. We have also arrested Moninder Singh after a detailed questioning. We have sealed the house and a thorough search is being carried out. We have also called two excavators to help the police in the search operations.'

LOOKING FOR ANSWERS

Local people were furious that the police had not acted earlier and there were two days of rioting. Under public pressure, six policemen were dismissed for dereliction of duty and two superintendents suspended.

It was noted that the corpses had been dissected with 'butcher-like precision'. In some cases, the torsos were missing. Police added that they were questioning Navin Choudhary, a medical store owner who had earlier been implicated in the possible sale of kidneys.

'We suspect that he was also involved in the crime. He has a past record and he was arrested in 1999 for being involved in an organ transplant racket,' said Rajesh Kumar Singh Rathore, senior superintendent of police.

It was alleged that the children had been killed for their kidneys, though this was discounted by a medical expert.

'Removal of the kidneys from a human body is a very delicate process and has to be necessarily done on a person with a beating heart, so that the blood circulation process is on. You cannot remove the kidney of a dead person,' said Diwakar Dalela, head of the urology department at King George's Medical University in Lucknow. 'Unless the kids were first taken to a well-equipped operation theatre for removal of kidneys and then done to death, the question of organ transplant could not arise. In any case, organ transplant requires so many pre-requisites like blood and kidney matching between the donor and recipient. Besides, no Indian hospital so far has facilities to preserve a kidney for more than three to four hours.'

Businessman Moninder Singh Pandher appears at a special CBI court in a case related to the gruesome Nithari killings. He was sentenced to death, although this was later overturned.

The media quickly found a new line of speculation. When erotic literature, along with a webcam and laptop, were found in Pandher's house he was immediately suspected of being involved in a child pornography ring. Pictures were unearthed of him with naked children. These turned out to be his grandchildren. Nothing linking him to paedophilia was ever discovered.

Most of the missing children were girls aged between three and 11. But the disappearances did not even make the news, although two children were going missing every month. This may have been because they were not locals. A majority of the 25,000 inhabitants of Nithari village were migrants from Uttar Pradesh, Bihar and West Bengal. They had come to Noida in search of work in the capital and the satellite towns in its periphery and earned their livelihoods as domestic helpers, drivers and fruit and vegetable vendors.

'We have been complaining about this for the past so many months but police only want money from us,' said one mother as she remembered the last time she saw her daughter who had been kidnapped 15 months earlier while playing outside her house. 'We only get abused and beaten by the cops every time we go to enquire about our missing children.'

The woman, Sunita, ran a makeshift laundry shop at the corner of the main road.

'Our worst fears have come true today,' said Pappu Lal, whose eight-year-old daughter Rachna Kumari went missing on 10 April 2006. 'We always suspected that something had happened to our children. I have gone to far off places like Jaipur, Mumbai, Bharatpur, Ajmer, Lucknow, Varanasi and Allahabad in search of our children.'

While Koli said Pandher had nothing to do with the murders, the police suspected he was merely trying to protect his employer. They were jailed in Mumbai, while India's Central Bureau of Investigation took over from the state police force.

MASTER AND SERVANT

Born in 1970, Surinder Koli dropped out from school at an early age. He did odd jobs before moving to Delhi, skinning animals for a living and sometimes eating the raw flesh. His first job in Delhi was to wash utensils at a rundown hotel. He then went to work as a cook for a retired brigadier in Noida. He left in 1998 to return to his village to get married, but within a month he left his wife and returned to Noida, where he worked for six years for a retired army major who introduced him to businessman Moninder Singh Pandher.

Pandher was 55 when he was arrested. His family and friends were shocked. They said he was a wonderful and amiable chap. He came from an affluent business family in Punjab, graduated from Delhi's prestigious St Stephen's College and inherited the successful family business. Everyone agreed that he was a most unlikely criminal.

However, investigators told a different story. They said he had a disturbed childhood and his marriage was a failure. His wife and son lived 240 km (150 miles) away in Chandigarh, though he visited them once in a while. He also travelled regularly to Los Angeles, Switzerland, Dubai, China and Canada, where his son studied, leaving Koli alone in his two-storey bungalow which was filled with fancy furniture, a collection of golf clubs and a cellar full of vintage wine. Pandher also used prostitutes, with Koli acting as a pimp.

However, both his wife and son stood up for him and Shanti Pandher denied media reports that she lived separately from her husband because of difficulties in their marriage.

'He is not guilty, not at all,' she said. 'This thing about children, it's rubbish. He is being framed. There's no truth in it.'

Pandher's 23-year-old son Karan claimed that his father had been convicted by the media without being given a fair trial.

'Do not accuse him right now. He is just a suspect,' he said. 'He is not a monster. Come on, have a heart. He has a family. He has a son.'

In an interview with the Zee News network, Karan Pandher said: 'If my father is found guilty – it's hard for me to say this – he should get the highest punishment. He should get capital punishment... The people of Nithari, children and my father need justice. But my father has not got a fair trial yet.'

Because of the case, their family business had suffered.

'Now no one wants to do business with us. I appeal to all that we are not bad people,' he said.

Koli and Pandher were both charged with kidnapping, raping and killing up to 38 women and children, then dismembering their bodies and dumping the remains into storm drains around Pandher's house. Koli continued to insist that he alone was guilty.

'Sahab did not know,' said Koli.

He told investigators that he committed the crimes while his master was away. Asked what he had done with the missing torsos of the victims, Koli disclosed that he ate some of the organs and cut up others and flushed them down the toilet. His first victim was a four-year-old girl. He admitted trying to eat the child's liver, but said he vomited immediately. According to the *Times of India*, Koli was trying to cure his impotence. He also admitted having sex with the dead bodies.

'I had always thought Surinder was behind all this,' said Karan. 'My father used to be out of town for long periods on business.'

However, on 12 February 2009, Koli and Pandher were both found guilty of the rape and murder of 14-year-old Rimpa Halder from a nearby slum, even though the judge Rama Jain conceded that Pandher was out of the country at the time of the murder. His passport and a statement from his wife showed that he was in Australia when Rimpa was killed.

Even though Pandher was out of the country, the judge maintained that he had entered into a criminal conspiracy with Koli to commit rape and murder.

In a statement to magistrates, Koli had said that he was more at peace in Pandher's absence as his homicidal tendencies remained at bay. The judge said that there was enough circumstantial evidence to convict Pandher. He lived in the house D-5 in Noida from 2004 until the serial killings were discovered in December 2006. Many murders had occurred during this period and human bones and skulls in polythene bags were recovered from the front and back of the house.

'Bones and skulls were recovered in such a mass scale from near a house which wasn't less than a slaughterhouse. The odour would have spread within a kilometre's radius,' said the judge, observing that it was highly unlikely Pandher would have been unaware that mass murder was happening inside his house.

'Before joining Pandher's house as a servant, Koli had earlier worked with several other households, but he committed this gruesome crime because Pandher brought call girls home and slept with more than two or three of them occasionally,' the judge said. 'Koli used to cook for all of them while Pandher would drink alcohol. All this brought out the worst criminal tendencies and sexual depravity of Koli, goading him to commit murders.'

Pronouncing sentence to a packed courtroom, Judge Jain held the crimes committed by Pandher and Koli to be the 'rarest of rare' and deserving of capital punishment. 'In the said case, a helpless, poor girl has been raped by the accused who resorted to extremely barbaric, inhuman and unkind acts which has no precedence. The manner in which the horrendous act has been carried out even puts that era into shame when humanity wasn't civilized,' she said, justifying the imposition of the maximum penalty. She rejected any calls for leniency.

'This crime is against womanhood and a blot on society,' Jain said. 'The manner in which the crime has been done, the death sentence can be the only justice because there was not an iota of indication that the convicts will mend their ways or reform their character in the future.'

Hearing the verdict, Pandher burst into tears while Koli seemed to remain unmoved.

However, on 11 September 2009, the Allahabad High Court acquitted Moninder Singh Pandher and set aside the death sentence given him by a lower court, but upheld the death sentence handed down to his domestic help Surinder Koli. Justice Imtiyaz Murtaza and Justice K.N. Pandey observed that 'no evidence has been placed on record to show that Pandher was guilty'.

Koli went on to be convicted on other counts. In May 2010, he was found guilty of murdering seven-year-old Arti Prasad and given a second death sentence. That September he was found guilty of murdering nine-year-old Rachna Lal and sentenced to death again. The following February he was given a fourth death sentence for the murder of 12-year-old Deepali Sarkar. Found guilty of the murder of five-year-old Chhoti Kavita, he was given a fifth death sentence, along with a life sentence for abduction, ten years for rape and seven for the destruction of evidence.

The Supreme Court also upheld the death sentence imposed on Koli, saying: 'In our opinion this case falls in the rarest of rare category and no mercy can be shown to him.'

He had given 'graphic details' of how he used to lure and kill young girls in Noida, the court said, 'The confessions had been made voluntarily before the magistrate and there is no defect in it.'

STEPHEN PORT

The Grindr Killer

USING A FALSE NAME and fake profile, Stephen Port used the gay dating app Grindr – along with Gaydar, FitLads, SlaveBoys, Hornet and Badoo – to pick up his victims. He used the names 'shyguy', 'top fun Joe', 'Basketballguy' and a variety of others, and cited his preference for slim men under 30. In one profile, he claimed to be an Oxford graduate; in another, a special needs teacher.

'I am a shy, polite guy. Enjoy keeping in shape, love to have a good time,' he said. 'I am romantic, caring and would take good care of my partner. I am successful, educated and determined. I'm looking for fun/ date/bf who is between 18–24, slim, smooth twink type, not too camp tho... who has plenty of energy and enjoys a good time.'

'Twinks' are young, boyish-looking men. It may not have been his intention at first to kill his pickups, but he liked to have sex with them when they were comatose and ended up overdosing them with the date-rape drug GHB.

AN IMMATURE SOUL

Port was brought up in Dagenham, Essex, England. At 16, he went to art college, but this proved too expensive for his parents – his father was a cleaner for the local council and his mother was a supermarket cashier. Instead, he spent two years training to be a chef. He found kitchen work at local businesses, events and weddings, before taking a

Stephen Port described himself as a shy, polite and romantic guy, but he was a deadly killer.

job at the Stagecoach bus depot in West Ham where he cooked for the drivers and staff.

He came out as gay in 2000 when he was 25 and in 2006 left home to move into a small flat in Cooke Street, Barking, where he was free to have parties and allow boyfriends to stay over. Living alone, he became increasingly selfish and hedonistic – cheating on partners, taking drugs, working as a male escort and eventually acting as a pimp for others. Friends remarked on his childishness. He would spend all day watching cartoons and would visit children's shops to buy toys, some of which would be placed above his bed.

He became a habitual user of gamma-Hydroxybutyric acid or GHB, which can be taken as a powder but is usually dissolved in water, and a colourless liquid called GBL, which is drunk and then converts into GHB in the body. In small doses it generates a feeling of euphoria, but only slightly larger amounts can cause unconsciousness and death. He also used amyl nitrite in the form of poppers, Viagra, mephedrone, also known as meow meow, and methamphetamine, or crystal meth.

With the rise of social media, he went out less and retreated into the online world. He joined, left, and rejoined social networks, sometimes using different names alongside his own picture, or creating entirely fictitious identities. On dating sites, he would seek out youthful-looking men, typically in their teens or early 20s – his so-called 'twinks'.

These were often vulnerable young men, some of whom turned to prostitution while having a volatile relationship with Port. He would advertise on escort sites, using his own phone number. One escort profile showed a young man naked and either unconscious or asleep on a bed.

Port also trawled the internet for 'date rape' pornography. The storyline of one of the pornographic videos he accessed featured drugs being slipped into a victim's drink. Soon Port would act this out in real life.

Early in 2012, a student in his late teens hooked up with Port through Grindr. They met at Barking station. The lad said Port 'was quite polite, friendly, nothing that would ring any alarm bells to me'.

They went back to Port's flat where he put on a cartoon video and gave the student a small glass of red wine which 'tasted bitter, which I attributed to it being cheap'.

After drinking the wine, he 'noticed a sludge in the bottom of the glass', then felt 'very dizzy and tired'. Port suggested he lie down in the bedroom, which he did alone and immediately fell asleep. When he woke, Port was raping him. After about a minute the student fell unconscious again. He awoke in the morning feeling 'disorientated'. Port drove him back to the station and chatted 'as if nothing had happened'. The student was too scared to say anything about what had occurred the previous night.

Early in the summer of 2014, Port picked up a young Muslim man on the Fitlads website. He visited Port's flat five times. On the first four occasions, nothing remarkable happened, but on the fifth Port plied him with drugs, though he had never consumed alcohol or drugs before. First, he tried poppers which, unusually, put him to sleep. When he awoke, Port gave him a clear liquid which he said was water.

'As soon as I drank it, I went unconscious,' the young man said. 'The next thing I remember I was on the floor screaming and shouting. It was like I was going mad.'

He found his underwear had been removed. Panic set in and he was desperate to get home. Port helped him get to Barking station.

'He was kind of dragging me along and holding me up,' the young man said.

Along the way, he started screaming and shouting again, vomited and was clearly in distress. At the station, the British Transport Police called an ambulance. But the Muslim man did not want the police involved in case his parents found out. They knew nothing of his sexuality. The police noted that Port was 'worried and jittery'. He claimed that the young man had turned up at his flat in his current state and he was merely helping him get home. There was no evidence that an offence had been committed and both men were allowed to go.

Two weeks later, on 17 June 2014, Port contacted 23-year-old fashion student Anthony Walgate, who occasionally worked as an escort, through the website Sleepyboys. Posing as a client and using the name Joe Dean, Port offered him £800 to spend the night with him. They met at Barking station at 10 pm and went back to Port's flat. Unbeknown to Port, Walgate had taken the precaution of texting a friend, giving the details of who he was meeting, along with a photograph Port had sent, jokingly saying: 'In case I get killed.'

At 4.18 am on 19 June, Port call an ambulance saying he had seen someone lying in Cooke Street, Barking, as he drove by.

'There's a young boy, looks like he's collapsed outside,' the caller said. He could have 'had a seizure or something, or just be drunk'.

Asked for his phone number, Port put the phone down, though the ambulance service phoned him back.

The police and an ambulance turned up to find a young man propped up against a wall. A doctor pronounced Walgate dead shortly before 8 am, although it was clear he had been dead for some hours. There were no signs of struggle or injury, but police noticed that the man's top was pulled up, exposing his midriff, as if he had been dragged there.

In a holdall next to the body, they found a brown bottle containing traces of GHB, and a post-mortem revealed high levels of GHB in his blood and urine within the range that death from GHB intoxication had been reported. His mobile phone was missing.

NOT GETTING HIS STORY STRAIGHT

When the police interviewed Port, he told a different story. He said he had got home after a night shift at about 4 am to find the man lying in front of his door and 'tried to rouse him by slapping his face'. The man made a 'gurgling' noise. He propped him against a wall and called an ambulance before going indoors.

The police quickly found he was lying. The details of his date that Walgate had left with his friend showed that the client he was visiting was Port. He was arrested on 26 June on suspicion of perverting the course of justice. They also suspected him of stealing Walgate's phone.

After two days' interrogation, Port changed tack. He asked detectives: 'Can I just say for the scenario – if it was an accident, and if he did have a fit in my place, is that still my fault?'

According to Port, Walgate had brought the drugs he had taken with him. They had sex twice. Walgate then said he was tired and was getting ready to leave when he collapsed on the bed still wearing his clothes and shoes. The following day Port said Walgate was snoring when he went to work. When he returned later that night, Walgate was still sleeping.

Port said that he woke at 3 am to find Walgate rigid, obviously dead, and panicked. The thought seized him: 'They're gonna think I murdered him or something.'

He took Walgate outside and went back to fetch his bag, saying he knew nothing about what had happened to his mobile phone. The police took samples of his DNA and seized a laptop from his house, though they failed to examine it. They then charged him with perverting the course of justice by giving a false statement to the police and bailed him.

While Barking police sought advice from a homicide assessment team, the case was not treated as murder. Despite the promptings of Walgate's friends at Middlesex University, the police did not examine Port's computer. If they had, they would have found that, minutes after assessing Walgate's escort profile on 13 June, he had conducted a series of searches on Google and pornography websites. Search terms included 'sleeping boy', 'unconscious boys', 'drugged and raped', 'taking date rape drug', 'gay teen knocked out raped' and 'guy raped and tortured young nude boy'.

'We had to badger them and almost feed them ideas,' college chum China Dunning said. 'I'd be like, "have you looked at his laptop"... and they'd be like "it's a really expensive procedure to do that".'

Kiera Brennan, another friend, said: 'They fobbed us off constantly... They kept saying "we're going to, we're going to" and then didn't. And every time we phoned the police officer at the time who was dealing with us he was either not there or someone would take a message and he'd never call us back.'

The case had not even gone to court when, on 28 August 2014, a woman walking her dog found the body of 22-year-old Gabriel Kovari propped up in a sitting position against the graveyard wall at St Margaret's Church, Barking, 500 yards (457 m) from Port's flat. Three weeks later, the same woman found the body of 21-year-old Daniel Whitworth propped up in a sitting position against the same graveyard wall. In his left hand, he had what appeared to be a suicide note. It said that Whitworth had killed himself with an overdose out of guilt because Kovari had died after taking drugs when they were having sex together.

THE POLICE ARE CALLED TO ACCOUNT

The police were convinced by this explanation. However, the coroner Nadia Persaud was not. She wanted to know why the police had not tested a blue bed sheet Whitworth had with him for DNA. Later, Port's DNA was found on it. Indeed, Port had written the suicide note, too, but the handwriting had not been compared to that in Whitworth's diary. A bottle of GHB found in a bag with his body was also later discovered to have Port's DNA in it, but was not tested at the time.

'My concerns of a third-party involvement in Daniel coming to be in the graveyard on 20 September cannot be allayed by the evidence that has been produced to the court,' she said. 'I cannot say beyond reasonable doubt that I am satisfied that he voluntarily took his own life. I also cannot say that I am satisfied that he was unlawfully killed.'

She was also concerned by bruises under Whitworth's armpits, and on his chest and neck, which she said suggested someone may have lifted him and moved him. An open verdict was recorded.

On 14 September the following year, the body of 25-year-old Jack Taylor was found in the same graveyard in the same position as the other two victims. All three were gay. In the intervening time, Port had served two months for perverting the course of justice in the Walgate case, though the prosecutor stressed: 'There is no suggestion that Mr Port bore any criminal responsibility for the death of the young man.'

Meanwhile, friends of Kovari and Whitworth had joined Walgrave's friends in putting pressure on the police and were drawing comparisons between the cases. They were then joined by the Taylor family, who discovered that there was CCTV footage of Jack walking down the street with a man a few hours before his death.

Although the police did not consider the death of Taylor suspicious, they published an image from the CCTV footage showing Taylor walking near Barking station with a tall, blond man, who was quickly identified as Stephen Port. He was arrested on 15 October 2015 and charged with all four murders three days later. He was convicted for the murders, as well as the rapes of three other men he had drugged, ten counts of administering a substance with intent and four sexual assaults, and was sentenced to life with a whole life tariff. An inquiry by the Independent Office of Police Conduct (IOPC) identified 'systemic failings' within the Metropolitan Police, but none of the 17 officers under investigation was disciplined.

HERB BAUMEISTER

The I-70 Strangler

THE I-70 HAS BEEN the killing ground of so many serial killers that it has become known as 'America's Sewer Pipe'. One killer who dumped the bodies of nine gay men along the stretch between Indianapolis and Columbus, Ohio, in the 1980s became known simply as the 'I-70 Strangler'. No suspect was ever apprehended, despite the widespread publicity the murders have generated, including their being featured several times on the television show *America's Most Wanted*.

However, in October 1998, authorities announced that they strongly suspected that Indianapolis businessman and serial killer Herb Baumeister could have been the I-70 Strangler. The remains of 11 other victims were scattered around the wooded area behind his ranch in Westfield, Indiana. But by the time they were unearthed, he was dead.

AN UNUSUAL LITTLE BOY

Born in 1947, Baumeister was the son of a doctor. As a child, he seemed normal enough, but by the time he reached adolescence it was plain that something was not quite right. He would fall into strange reveries and ponder what it was like to taste human urine. When he found a dead crow in the road, he took it to school and dropped it on his teacher's desk when she wasn't looking. His father took him for psychological tests. He was diagnosed with schizophrenia, though there was no record of treatment for the condition.

As a child, Baumeister seemed normal enough, but when he was taken for psychological tests he was diagnosed with schizophrenia.

He dropped out of college and his father got him a job as a copyboy on the *Indianapolis Star*. Though he tried to fit in, he was generally considered an oddball. In 1971, he married college graduate Juliana Saitor in the United Methodist Church in Indiana. They were both Young Republicans and both yearned to own their own business one day. Six months after they were married, Baumeister spent two months in a psychiatric hospital.

Baumeister got a well-paid job at the Bureau of Motor Vehicles and Juliana quit working as a high-school journalism instructor to become a stay-at-home mother. Over the next five years, they had three children. But Baumeister was a closet homosexual. Juliana said; over the 25 years of their marriage, they only had sex six times. She had never even seen her husband naked. Seemingly ashamed of his skinny body – in front of a woman, at least – he put his pyjamas on in the bathroom before coming to bed.

His behaviour at the Bureau of Motor Vehicles became increasingly odd. He sent Christmas cards showing himself and another man dressed in drag. Nevertheless, he was promoted to program director and his employment was only terminated when, bizarrely, he urinated on a letter addressed to the governor. The ever-loyal Juliana went back to work to support the family, while he got a job in a thrift shop. Around that time, the body of 17-year-old Eric Roetiger was found dumped along Interstate 70.

Baumeister found himself in trouble with the police over an auto-theft and a hit-and-run while he was drunk. He beat the rap. Then his father died and he borrowed $4,000 from his mother to open a thrift shop of his own in conjunction with the Children's Bureau of Indianapolis. With Juliana's help, in the first year it earned $50,000. Soon they opened the second in their Sav-A-Lot thrift-store chain. Meanwhile, the body of 27-year-old Steven Elliot was found along I-70 in 1989 and that of 32-year-old Clay Boatman in 1990. Six more would follow.

GOING UP IN THE WORLD

Now a successful business couple, the Baumeisters moved into the $1-million mock-Tudor Fox Hollow Farm in the fashionable Westfield suburb, some 32 km (20 miles) from Indianapolis. It had four bedrooms, an indoor swimming pool in the basement, a riding stable and 18-and-a-half acres (7.5 hectares) of grounds. The Strangler then ceased dumping his victims along the I-70.

Unbeknown to his wife, Baumeister secretly frequented gay bars in Indianapolis. In the summer, when Juliana and the kids were away at his mother's lakeside condominium, he would invite young men back for a 'cocktail and a swim' at Fox Hollow Farm. During sex, he would strangle them, then burn their bodies and scatter their bones in the grounds.

Ten men went missing over two years, leaving no clues as to their whereabouts. The police took little interest, so the mother of 28-year-old Alan Broussard went to see private detective Virgil Vandagriff. Her son had last been seen leaving a gay bar called Brothers on 6 June 1994. Vandagriff was not greatly concerned. There could be an innocent explanation for his disappearance. Nevertheless, he had posters printed asking for information from anyone who had seen Alan.

Then Vandagriff discovered that a detective named Mary Wilson at the missing person's bureau was working on the disappearance of other gay men of similar ages and physical appearance. He also came across an article in the gay lifestyle magazine *Indiana Word* about 31-year-old Jeff Jones who had disappeared in July 1993. Vandagriff was researching these cases when 34-year-old Roger Goodlet vanished after he had left his mother's house to visit a gay bar.

'The fates of these three men were too close to ignore,' said Vandagriff. He was convinced a serial killer was at work.

A friend of Goodlet's, who knew him from the gay scene, saw one of Vandagriff's posters and got in touch, saying that he had been picked up by a man who called himself Brian Smart. They had gone to Smart's sprawling estate for a drink and a swim.

After swimming naked in the basement pool, Smart said: 'I just learned this really neat trick. If you choke someone while you're having sex it feels really great. You really get a great rush.'

Indicating the carotid arteries in his neck, he said: 'You just want to pinch these two veins. And it's such a great buzz. You should see how someone looks when you're doing it to them. Their lips change colour – that's how you can tell it's working.'

Smart raved about erotic asphyxiation.

'Do it to me,' he begged. He lay back on a couch and masturbated while being throttled.

When it came time to swap roles, the informant feigned unconsciousness while being throttled. Finding the man he had just choked still alive, Smart grew agitated and admitted that, sometimes, there had been accidents. When he asked about Roger Goodlet, his host grew defensive. Nevertheless, he managed to persuade Smart to give him a lift back to Indianapolis. He told the police about the incident, but they treated him like he was crazy.

Vandagriff took his informant to meet Mary Wilson. She was also investigating the disappearance of 20-year-old Richard Hamilton, 21-year-old Johnny Bayer and 28-year-old Allan Livingstone who had gone missing the previous year, as well as other persons dating back to the early 1990s. All of them were gay.

There was little they could do with the information that Vandagriff's informant had brought them. There were many places in the Westfield area that matched the informant's description and Brian Smart proved to be a pseudonym. All they could do was hope that he would turn up again on the gay scene.

SPIRALLING OUT OF CONTROL

Meanwhile, the fortunes of the Sav-A-Lot stores were in a steep decline. Baumeister was frequently drunk and fired employees on a whim. The

Children's Bureau withdrew its support and Juliana was contemplating divorce. Then their son, 13-year-old Erich, found a human skeleton in the backyard. Baumeister insisted that it had belonged to his father's medical practice. He had come across it when he had been clearing out the garage and had thrown it away.

On 29 August 1995, Vandagriff's informant spotted the man he knew as Brian Smart again in a gay bar and took down his licence-plate number when he left. The car was registered to Herbert R. Baumeister of Fox Hollow Farm, Westfield, Indiana.

Mary Wilson and Lieutenant Thomas Green approached Baumeister in his shop. They told him that they were investigating the disappearance of several young men and asked for permission to search his home. When he refused, they petitioned his wife who was co-owner of the property. They told Juliana that her husband cruised gay bars and that they suspected him of being a serial killer. She refused to believe them.

'The police came to me and said, "We are investigating your husband in relation to homosexual homicide,"' she recalled. 'I remember saying to them, "Can you tell me what homosexual homicide is?"'

Wilson then tried to get a search warrant. But Westfield is in Hamilton County, outside the jurisdiction of the Indianapolis police, the city being in Marion County. And the authorities in Hamilton County refused to co-operate.

The Sav-A-Lot stores were failing and the Baumeisters filed for divorce. Juliana began to fear for her husband's sanity and felt released from any duty of loyalty to him. In June 1996, when he was away, she got in touch with Mary Wilson and told her about the skeleton Erich had found.

Wilson visited Fox Hollow Farm with two detectives from the Hamilton County Sheriff's office. On a brief inspection of the Baumeisters' estate, they found numerous fragments of charred bones and teeth. Over the next three months, they found the remains of an estimated 11 men, only four of whom were positively identified.

All the victims used the same bars that Baumeister visited and disappeared at times when his wife and kids were away. Meanwhile, 49-year-old Baumeister himself disappeared. On 3 July 1996, campers found his body lying beside his car in Ontario's Pinery Provincial Park. He had a bullet hole in his forehead and a .357 Magnum in his hand. He left a suicide notice that mentioned his failing business and marriage, but nothing about the murders.

An FBI profiler said that Baumeister's cavalier manner of openly dumping his victims' corpses on his own land indicated that he had killed many times before. Baumeister had insinuated to a potential victim that he had killed 50 to 60 people, though he may have been bragging. He was known to have travelled on the I-70 from Indiana to Ohio around the time of the highway killings, which stopped in 1991, around the time that Baumeister bought Fox Hollow Farm.

In 1998, investigators concluded that Baumeister probably killed 60 men in all after linking him to nine other men whose bodies were found dumped along the I-70 in Indiana and Ohio between 1980 and 1990. Baumeister's wife provided credit card receipts, phone call records, and even gave the police the use of the car that her husband had used on those business trips.

Baumeister's photo matched the police sketch drawn from descriptions provided by witnesses who thought they had seen the I-70 Strangler. One eyewitness identified Baumeister's picture as the same man who had given his friend Michael Riley a lift home from a bar one evening in 1988. Riley was found dead the next morning.

'We'll never know for sure, of course, if he was indeed the same man,' said Virgil Vandagriff. 'Everything points to him – even the fact that the roadside killings ended at the same time he bought his house and now had a place with plenty of room to dump his bodies with a lot less hassle.'

However, Vandagriff complained that, as a private detective, he did not always have the freedom or the money to follow his suspicions to their conclusion.

'I would have taken the Baumeister case a lot further than I feel the police did,' he said. 'While there were many fine moments in the investigation... I think there were certain loose ends that should have been tied up.'

For example, while Baumeister was active in Fox Hollow Farm, his older brother in Texas was found dead in his pool.

PORTRAIT OF A SERIAL KILLER

Vandagriff found time to write a report called *Who Is A Serial Killer?* which offers an insight into the Baumeister case. Describing the typical serial killer, he said: 'He is typically white, male, between the ages of 25 and 35. He is often married, has children and has full-time employment. The majority of the time he will kill white victims.... His intellect ranges from below average to above average. He does not know his victims nor have any particular hatred for them.

'Of the four main types of killers – the psychotic, the missionary motive type, the thrill killer and the lust killer, Baumeister fits the last category. The lust killer, the most common type, gets turned on by the killings. They usually torture their victims. The more heinous their action the more they become aroused.

'Serial killers experience certain traumas in life. These are many. Among them are those suffered by Baumeister: poor body image (witnessed by the fact he didn't want his wife to see his lanky body nude) and phobias (over-concerned about what his co-workers thought of him at the *Indianapolis Star* and at the BMV).

'Herb also had feelings of what is called disassociation, including separation of feelings (able to kill and then go on to live a normal life with his children) and daydreaming...

'Often, there is trauma re-enforcement; in Herb's case this translates as loss of employment and financial stress brought on by the decline of the Sav-A-Lot stores. Facilitators, such as alcohol and drugs, seem to have served as accessories to Herb's crimes.... In short, Herbert Richard Baumeister was the consummate serial killer.'

ROBERT CHARLES BROWNE

Seven Virgins

IN 1991, 13-YEAR-OLD HEATHER Dawn Church was abducted from her home in Black Forest, Colorado, while she was babysitting. Two years later her skull was found in nearby mountains. Fingerprints had been found on the window ledge of her bedroom. They matched those of Robert Charles Browne, who had served time in Louisiana for car theft in 1987. When he was finally arrested in March 1995, he denied the murder, but pleaded guilty in court to avoid the death penalty. He was sentenced to life without parole and that seemed to be the end of that.

However, he sent a cryptic letter to the prosecutors. 'Seven sacred virgins, entombed side by side, those less worthy, are scattered wide,' the letter read. 'The score is you 1, the other team 48. If you were to drive to the end zone in a white Trans Am, the score could be 9 to 48.'

He attached a hand-drawn map listing numbers of victims in different states – seven in Texas, nine in Colorado, 17 in Louisiana, three in Mississippi, five in Arkansas, two each for California, Oklahoma and New Mexico, and one in Washington state. Cold-case investigators across those states went to work and found that many of his assertions were credible, though it was thought that he was claiming 49 murders in order to challenge Gary Ridgway's record.

Robert Charles Browne admitted to at least 48 killings across the USA.

'It's possible he's exaggerating, but I don't think you can conduct business assuming he's exaggerating,' El Paso County Sheriff Terry Maketa said. 'We'll continue to pursue leads.'

Deputies complained that Browne was taunting them, but former FBI and CIA agent Charlie Hess, a sheriff's department cold-case investigator, set up a correspondence with him.

'We started by writing a very direct letter to Robert indicating who we were,' said Hess. 'It became obvious with Robert that most things were a negotiation: If I can have a single cell I'll tell you this. If I can have this, I can give you three murders,' said Hess. 'All of the things he asked for were reasonable, within the law, within the rules of DOC [Department of Corrections].'

Hess added: 'He told me outright, "Get me a private doctor, I'll give you three murders."' Hess complied and Browne gave up details that only the killer could have known.

On 27 July 2006, Browne pleaded guilty to first-degree murder and received another life sentence for the murder of 15-year-old Rocio Delpilar Sperry on 10 November 1987 at an apartment complex in Colorado Springs. He strangled her. Afterwards, he dismembered her body in the bathtub, 'just popping' her joints apart, as he remembered. He said he had dumped her body in a rubbish bin. It was never found.

She was the wife of a soldier and the mother of a three-month-old girl. Her husband lost custody of his baby daughter after his family blamed him for the murder of his teenage wife. He later said that Browne's guilty plea had brought him a measure of peace after two decades of grief.

'Last week was the first time I had a dream about my wife,' he said. 'It was her face, and there was a bright light behind it. I woke up and I felt good. I feel I can move on.'

Heather Church's father Mike said: 'I can identify with him and I'm so very thankful for the closure that he has with his family and his daughter.'

A YOUNG MAN WITH A SHORT FUSE

Robert Browne was born in 1952 in Coushatta, Louisiana, a town of fewer than 3,000 inhabitants some 80 km (50 miles) south-west of Shreveport. He was the youngest of nine children, including three sets of twins. His parents ran the local dairy.

'He came from a tough family,' said the sheriff. 'They came up during some hard times.'

His high school teacher said that Browne was competitive and had a temper, but wasn't too different from most kids.

'I remember him being kind of a loner, but not somebody you would expect to do this. He wasn't one that had a lot of friends, but he had friends,' he said. 'He did have a hot temper. In a pickup basketball game, if somebody fouled him or hit him, he'd fly off the handle.'

Although he had an IQ of 140, Browne dropped out of school and at the age of 17 joined the US Army and served in South Korea where, he claimed, he killed a man in a fight over a prostitute. The murder remained unverified. Serving from 1969 to 1976, he attained the rank of sergeant before being dishonourably discharged for a drug offence.

Browne had a series of six wives or 'what he would consider a wife', according to El Paso District Attorney John Newsome. All six were similar in appearance – petite, weighing between 43–57 kg (95–125 lb) – and all six were still alive when he was convicted for murder.

One of them, Rita Morgan, met Browne when she was 16 and he was still serving overseas. They exchanged letters. When they next met she was recently divorced with two boys, and in her 20s. She was working as a waitress at the Cotton Patch in Coushatta. He remembered her right away, brought her flowers and asked her out.

'He made you feel comfortable, like you knew him,' Morgan said. In 1980 she became his fourth wife, but the marriage was not a week old before he changed. 'I could just kill you, and nobody would do anything about it down here,' he told her.

The man who had once held open the car door for her would knock her down for losing a set of keys. Though he apologized and said it would never happen again, she never knew what might send him into a rage. When her father tried to talk to him, Browne told him to mind his own business, and said that he would 'do whatever I want, whenever I want'.

Rita witnessed other violence. She said she saw Browne punch his mother for refusing to give him money. He choked her so hard that she had to go to hospital, and he once pointed a gun at her head. He pulled the trigger, but the gun didn't fire.

'It's not your day, is it?' he said. Then he asked her to take the gun and shoot him.

'Do it yourself,' she said.

After a rocky marriage where they separated regularly, she left for good when he hurt her son.

'That's what did it,' she said. 'He had no concern. You might hurt me, but the day it involved my children and you're not helping me.... He never even called up to the hospital.'

They divorced in 1984 after four years of marriage. Even so, their marriage had lasted longer than his other relationships and he had been killing women while they were together. Nor was he apologetic about it.

'Women are unfaithful, they screw around a lot, they cheat, and they are not of the highest moral value,' he told detectives. 'They cheat and they are users.'

A MAN WITHOUT A PLAN

He told investigators he rarely if ever planned a killing, choosing his prey at random. He met his victims in everyday settings – a motel bar, a restaurant, a convenience store or apartment block where he worked. He said he never just went out 'looking for someone'. His motive? 'It was just disgust with the person and some of it just confrontation.'

Investigators were confused because he used different types of guns and strangled, stabbed and sometimes beat his victims. One died after he put a rag soaked in ant killer over her face while she slept, he said. Sheriff Maketa said Browne probably got away with his crimes because he never spent much time with his victims before killing them and was adept at disposing of their bodies.

His first known victim was 15-year-old Katherine Hayes who disappeared after leaving Fausto's restaurant in Coushatta on 4 July 1980. Hayes' body was found in October in Nantachie Creek. Browne said he had taken her to a house, had sex with her and strangled her with shoelaces.

Twenty-six-year-old Faye Self was reported missing 30 March 1983 after she left the Wagon Wheel bar on Louisiana Highway 1. She said she was going to pick up her daughter and had to get home because she had work the following day. However, she left her car at the bar. Browne told authorities that he went to Self's apartment, which was next to his. He said he placed a chloroform-soaked rag over her face and left to get rope to tie her up, but she died before he could have sex with her. He said he disposed of her body in the Red River, which was near the apartment building. Her body was never found. Her daughter Tiffany was just 11 months old when her mother disappeared. She had two older children.

Twenty-one-year-old Wanda Faye Hudson was found dead on 28 May 1983, in her apartment in Coushatta. She had been restrained with an ant pesticide that contained chloroform and stabbed multiple times with a screwdriver. Browne was living in the same block and had done maintenance work on Hudson's apartment, including changing the lock on her door the day before she died. At the time, the block belonged to his brother Donald and his father Ronald was a deputy on the team investigating the murder.

Twenty-two-year-old Melody Bush was found dead on 30 March 1984, in Flatonia Fayette County, Texas. Her body was found in a drainage ditch and the coroner ruled Bush died of acute acetone poisoning. This was puzzling as acetone, used as nail polish, paint remover and drain unblocker, would normally be vomited up before a lethal dose could be ingested. The police first suspected her husband Robert. The couple had been seen drinking and arguing in the Antlers Inn's Stag Bar at the back of the hotel in Flatonia, where she was last seen. However, the police never found any evidence to link him to the killing.

Melody was barefoot and so drunk she was having trouble walking when she left the bar. Browne variously claimed he had picked her up in the bar or at the side of the road – others said she left the bar alone. He said he had taken her back to his motel room. After they had sex, Browne told Hess: 'Then I used ether on her. Put her out. And then I used an ice pick on her. She was just acting like a slutty, low-life woman.'

He then said he returned to the bar, then visited a local truck stop with a bartender to have breakfast. When he went back to his motel room, her body was still lying on the bed. He loaded her body into his van and then drove north of Flatonia and dumped the body over a bridge. Melody's body was found in a culvert five days later. Browne told investigators in Colorado that at the time of Bush's murder, he was employed as a truck driver and delivered flowers. One of his routes took him through Flatonia.

He was in Texas again on 2 February 1984 when 17-year-old Nidia Mendoza went missing. Her remains were found four days later in a ditch. Browne had cut off her head and legs using a dull butcher's knife he found in his motel kitchenette.

Investigators concluded that she had left the Dames nightclub and gone back to the Embassy Suite, where they had sex. He then strangled her and cut her up in the bath.

'Mr Browne indicated he actually dismembered the body and put the pieces in a suitcase,' said Captain Gary Cox of the Sugar Land Police Department. 'He actually walked through the hotel with the suitcase, emptied the contents into the van, then went back to the room to get the additional body parts.'

The month following the murder of Heather Church, 21-year-old Lisa Lowe was reported missing on 3 November in Arkansas. She disappeared as she was going to a club in Forrest City. She dropped off her children at their aunt's apartment, and was going to walk the three or four blocks to the club. She never arrived.

Her badly decomposed body was found on 26 November in the St Francis River. She had been strangled. She left four young children, who were raised by their grandmother and aunts. Until Browne's confession, the main suspect had been their father, though no evidence had been found linking him to her death.

Other investigations are still ongoing.

'We don't like to call them cold cases,' said Hess. 'We like to call them unresolved cases. A cold case would indicate to me a case that is put on the shelf and forgotten. We don't forget them.'

CHAPTER TWENTY-ONE

DAVID CARPENTER

The Trailside Killer

ON 19 AUGUST 1979, 44-year-old bank executive Edda Kane went out for a hike along the trails at the foot of Mount Tamalpais which overlooks San Francisco's Golden Gate Bridge. When she did not return home, her husband called the police. The following day they found her with a .44 bullet in the back of her head. She had been on her knees and possibly forced to show her killer some sort of obeisance when she was shot. She had not been raped and, although $10 was missing from her wallet along with some credit cards, the killer had left her jewellery.

Another murder took place in Mount Tamalpais State Park on 8 March the following year. This time there was a witness. A woman hiker was standing in the trees when she saw a man approach 23-year-old Barbara Schwartz. Suddenly he pulled out a knife and stabbed her repeatedly in the chest. The eyewitness said he was about 25, though she later admitted that she was mistaken. Others said they saw a suspicious man in his 40s in the vicinity. He had been wearing a raincoat, though there was no sign of rain.

A 25 cm (10 in) boning knife was found nearby, but a TV reporter had picked it up, smudging any fingerprints. It came from a grocery chain, but it was impossible to determine which store. A pair of glasses were also found. They were prison issue. The police checked the description the eyewitness gave against recently released sex offenders.

Twenty-six-year-old Anne Alderson was seen jogging on 15 October 1980 near where Edda Kane had been killed. When her body was found, she had a .38 bullet in her right temple. She, too, had been kneeling when she was killed. However, she had been raped, but had been allowed to get dressed before she was executed.

On 28 November 25-year-old Shauna May was supposed to meet friends in Point Reyes National Seashore Park, 32 km (20 miles) further north, to go hiking. She did not turn up. Two days later her naked body was found dumped in a shallow trench. She had been trussed with wire, raped and shot in the head three times.

Next to her was the body of 22-year-old Diana O'Connell, who had gone missing when out on the trail with friends. She had been shot in the head. Their clothes had been stuffed into their knapsacks and a pair of panties had been stuffed into Diana's mouth.

Two more bodies were found nearby. These belonged to 19-year-old Richard Stowers and his 18-year-old fiancée Cynthia Moreland. They had gone out hiking seven weeks earlier and had been reported missing on 11 October, just a few days before Anne Alderson had gone missing. There was speculation that the Zodiac Killer, who had killed at least seven people in northern California in the late 1960s, was on the loose again.

FBI profiler John Douglas was called in. He said that the killer was a local man – white, intelligent, blue collar and had spent time in jail. He had raped before, but not killed. His history would include bed-wetting, cruelty to animals and, possibly, fire-starting. Douglas also believed that he had a speech impediment. This was because he did not pick up his victims in a social situation, but approached them from behind and overwhelmed them to give himself a sense of compensation for his handicap.

The next killing took place near Santa Cruz, some 128 km (80 miles) south of San Francisco. On 29 March 1981, 20-year-old Ellen Marie Hansen and her boyfriend Stephen Haertle, both undergraduates at the University of California at Davis, were attacked while hiking in the Henry Cowell Redwoods State Park. Haertle survived and said that a man had approached them with a gun in his hand and said he was going to rape Ellen. She refused to co-operate and Haertle begged the man to let them go. The man then shot Ellen point blank in the head. He then shot Haertle in the neck and made off.

Badly wounded, Haertle sought help from other hikers. Though suffering from trauma, he managed to give a description of the attacker to police. He was 178–183 cm (5 ft 10 in–6 ft) tall, weighed about 77 kg (170 lb) and was about 50 and balding. Wearing dark glasses and a gold jacket, he had crooked yellow teeth. Others on the trail saw him make off in a red car. One of them thought it was a Fiat.

A drawing made from Haertle's description was printed in local newspapers. A reader identified him as the purser on a ship she had sailed on to Japan who had behaved inappropriately towards her daughter 26 years earlier. His name had been David Carpenter. However, there were many men named David Carpenter in northern California. As a precaution, the killer began growing a beard and began hunting – fatefully – closer to home.

Twenty-year-old Heather Roxanne Scaggs was an intern at Econo Quick Print where Carpenter taught students how to use the new computerized typesetting machines. He sometimes gave her a lift home. When she said she wanted to have a car of her own, Carpenter said he would help her. He had a friend who was trying to sell a vehicle. She told her boyfriend Dan Pingle about it, giving him Carpenter's address. When she did not return, he went to confront Carpenter, who claimed that he had not met up with Heather that morning. Pingle then contacted the police.

While Carpenter had served time in jail, he had been released from the state penitentiary into federal custody, so he did not show up on the list of those freed. And although the crimes he had been convicted of clearly had a sexual motivation, they were not technically sex crimes, so he had eluded the investigation earlier.

COMMUNICATION BREAKDOWN

Fifty-one-year-old David Joseph Carpenter still lived with his aged parents. The police and the FBI put him under surveillance. Then, when he met other criminals, in violation of his parole conditions, they arrested him.

'Please don't hurt me,' he said and insisted on getting a lawyer.

Haertle and several other witnesses picked him out of a lineup. Witnesses also identified his car with its distinctive bent tailpipe. A former fiancée said that he had a gold jacket which he said he had lost around the time of the Hansen murder. And in his house, the police found local hiking guides and over 60 maps showing trails where the victims had perished. The police also recovered the .38. Carpenter had given it to a friend who was a bank robber. He suspected that Carpenter was trying to set him up and wanted no part of it.

Carpenter was formally charged with the murder of Ellen Hansen and the attempted murder of Stephen Haertle. At his arraignment it was clear that he had a debilitating speech impediment. His stutter was so bad that he could not answer the judge's questions, barely being able to agree that the name in the indictment was correct.

'Carpenter's face contorted and his head shook as he struggled to respond,' said one court reporter. 'He finally managed to utter a "yes" after the passage of several seconds.'

The remains of Heather Scaggs were found hidden under some brush in the Big Basin Redwoods Park to the south of San Francisco on 24 May. She had been raped and shot through the eye with a .38. Her clothes and possessions, except for one earring, had been taken.

Five more murder charges were laid in Marin County that covers Mount Tamalpais State Park and Point Reyes National Seashore Park.

However, charges for the murders of Edda Kane and Barbara Schwartz were not filed as a different gun had been used in the Kane case and Schwartz had been stabbed.

Carpenter's history was studied, not least by John Douglas as criminal profiling was then in its infancy. He had been born in San Francisco in 1930 to a domineering mother and an alcoholic father who alternately beat and neglected him. By seven, he had developed a painful stutter. Ridiculed at school, he became withdrawn, wetting the bed and torturing animals – two out of Douglas' key indicators.

At 17 he was arrested for molesting two young cousins and spent a year in the custody of the California Youth Authority. He took various jobs, including being a ship's purser, a printer and a salesman. In 1955, at the age of 25, he married and quickly fathered three children. This did little to assuage his raging sexual appetite and he prowled around at night, looking for other women, often flying into violent rages.

In 1960, he befriended a woman, even inviting her home. She became a friend of the family until, one day, he drove her to a wooded area, tied her up and threatened her with a knife. During the incident, Carpenter lost his stutter. When the woman resisted he struck her with a hammer. A military police officer heard her cries and intervened. Carpenter shot at him. He returned fire, wounding Carpenter.

Although Carpenter claimed to have blacked out during the attack, he was sentenced to 14 years. His wife seized the opportunity to divorce him. He was released after nine years and quickly remarried. That marriage failed, too. He then tried to rape a woman he had dragged from a car. He stabbed her, but she managed to get away and find help. While awaiting trial, he broke out of jail with four other inmates. They were quickly recaptured and he was sentenced to another nine years.

He got out in May 1979. Edda Kane was killed in August. Meanwhile, Carpenter had taken a job as a typesetter and took up hiking as a hobby.

On 16 June, while Carpenter was in custody, rock climbers found a human jawbone in Castle Rock State Park to the south of San Francisco. It belonged to 17-year-old high school student Anna Kelly Menjivar, who had been missing since 28 December the previous year. She had worked part-time in a bank which Carpenter used and it was noted that he took an interest in her. However, the cause of death could not be established and the evidence connecting Carpenter to her death was thin.

A 'MENTAL MESS' FACES JUSTICE

As feelings were running high in northern California, the trial for the murders of Heather Scaggs and Ellen Hansen, and the attempted murder of Stephen Haertle, was moved to Los Angeles. He pleaded not guilty. The trial lasted six weeks and, on 6 July 1984, Carpenter was convicted of two counts of first-degree murder and one count of attempted murder. Although his attorney described Carpenter as a 'mental mess' and insisted that there had been no premeditation, he was sentenced to death in the gas chamber at San Quentin because of two aggravating factors: rape and the fact that he had lain in wait for his victims.

The second trial for the Marin County murders opened in San Diego on 5 January 1988. The prosecution called 60 witnesses, the defence 30 and Carpenter himself took the stand.

Testifying for seven days, he appeared calm and prepared, reading from his calendar and his collection of receipts in an attempt to establish alibis. He stuttered occasionally when describing fellow inmates and his relationships with women. Otherwise, he let flashes of anger show through and generally appeared glib. The prosecution easily demolished his alibis, showing that he had altered the documentation or had simply got the date wrong.

Carpenter was convicted of all five murders and sentenced to death once more. However, a few months after the trial, the forewoman of the

David Carpenter watches television in his cell on death row, San Quentin.

jury revealed that she had been aware of Carpenter's convictions in Los Angeles in 1984 for the Santa Cruz murders. She had not mentioned this during the *voir dire* – the pre-trial examination of the jury – and the judge had no option but to declare a mistrial, though he was satisfied that the evidence of Carpenter's guilt was overwhelming.

The state prosecutors took the matter to the California Supreme Court who ruled that the forewoman's knowledge had not unduly biased the jury and overturned the judge's decision. The California Supreme Court also upheld both death sentences, though Carpenter still awaits execution on death row in San Quentin.

Chapter Twenty-two

KENNETH ERSKINE

The Stockwell Strangler

When 78-year-old Nancy Emms was found dead in her basement flat in West Hill Road in the south London borough of Wandsworth on 9 April 1986, there were no signs of foul play. A doctor called to the scene thought she had lain there for about three days and signed a death certificate saying she had died from natural causes. Then the home help noticed that her portable TV was missing.

The police were called and a post-mortem found that she had been strangled and sodomized. There was also bruising around her ribs as if someone had knelt on her chest. There was no sign of a forced entry, but it was known that Mrs Emms often slept with the window open. There was only one clue to the identity of the killer. A curly hair was found, thought to have come from the head of an Afro-Caribbean.

Two months later, on 9 June, the body of 69-year-old Janet Cockett was found in her first-floor flat in Warwick House, 8 km (5 miles) away on the Overton Estate in the Stockwell district of south London. This time there had clearly been foul play. Her nightdress had been ripped from her body, though it was left neatly folded on a chair beside the bed. She had been strangled and sexually assaulted, and two of her ribs were broken as the result of heavy pressure rather than a blow.

Strangely, the family photographs on her mantelpiece were turned away from the scene of the crime. The killer had made no effort to hide his identity. There was a fresh palm print on the bathroom window where, the police concluded, the intruder had got in. It was a warm night and the window had been left open.

In the early hours of 27 June 73-year-old retired engineer Fred Prentice was asleep in the Bradmead old people's home in Cedars Road, Clapham, a south London borough abutting Stockwell, when he was woken by footsteps in the corridor outside. He saw a shadow against the frosted glass of his bedroom door. A young man entered, ran to the bed and jumped on top of him.

'I was absolutely petrified,' said Prentice, 'but there was nothing I could do. He was sitting on my chest with his fingers clutching my neck. I thought I was a goner.'

The stranger who was strangling him hissed over and over: 'Kill, kill, kill...' Fighting for his life, Fred reached for the alarm button at the head of the bed and pushed it. His attacker let go and fled.

The police were puzzled. It was unusual for a killer to attack both men and women, yet there were clearly parallels between the crimes. Confirmation that they were the work of a serial killer came the very next night when the bodies of 84-year-old Valentine Gliem and 94-year-old Polish-born Zbigniew Stabrawa were found dead in their adjoining rooms at Somerville Hastings House, an old people's home in Stockwell Park Crescent. Both men had been strangled manually and sexually assaulted.

One of the night staff had seen an intruder creeping along the corridor and called the police, but the man had vanished before they arrived. Once more the killer had gained entrance through an open window. With five attacks in the area, the newspapers quickly dubbed him the Stockwell Strangler.

Scotland Yard's Detective Chief Superintendent Ken Thompson was put in charge of a task force of 200 detectives to find the culprit. Dozens of plainclothes officers were sent to guard old people's homes across south London. However, the killer wrong-footed them by striking next north of the river.

On 9 July, 82-year-old William Carmen was found dead in his bed in Sybil Thorndike House on the Marquess Estate in Islington. He had been strangled, molested and £400 that the old man was known to have kept in his bedroom was missing. Although it was a hot summer, the elderly were warned to keep their windows closed at night. But still the killing went on.

Three days later, 75-year-old Trevor Thomas was found dead in the bath at his home in Barton Court, Clapham. He had been dead for some time, so there was little forensic evidence. While he was not officially counted as a victim of the Stockwell Strangler, he was thought to have been one.

The killer returned to the Overton Estate in Stockwell on 20 July. Seventy-four-year-old William Downes was found dead in his bedsit in Hollies House. He had been strangled and sexually assaulted.

'I warned him to keep his door and windows locked, especially at night,' said his son. 'But it was hot and I think he left just one slightly open to let some air in.'

That was enough for the Strangler. However, the attack gave the police fresh leads. Palm prints found on the gate and kitchen wall matched the one left in Janet Cockett's home. The problem was that, while fingerprint records had been computerized, work digitizing palm prints had not even begun, so checking this one against the records was a mammoth task. There were a staggering four million prints to go through. The job was reduced to a manageable size by concentrating on London-based burglars and petty thieves. This gave the Strangler time to strike again.

On 24 July, 80-year-old Florence Tisdall was found dead in her flat in Ranelagh Gardens near Putney Bridge. She had been strangled, sexually assaulted and had broken ribs where the killer had knelt on the frail old woman's chest.

HOMELESS AND HOPELESS

From the palm prints, the police knew they were looking for 24-year-old Kenneth Erskine. Born to an English mother and an Antiguan father, who then divorced, Erskine was brought up in Putney where he was remembered as a chubby, Bible-reading boy. However, he was difficult to control and was sent to a school for maladjusted children. There, Erskine inhabited a fantasy world, where he assumed the role of Lawrence of Arabia, attacking and tying up smaller, weaker children.

Homicidal tendencies manifested themselves early. Erskine tried to drown other children on trips to the swimming pool, holding their heads under water until staff intervened. On one occasion, he attacked a teacher, stabbing him in the hand with a pair of scissors. A psychiatric nurse who tried to examine him was taken hostage when he held a pair of scissors to her throat. Whenever female staff tried to show him affection, he would shock them by rubbing himself against them, or exposing his genitals.

Leaving school at 16, Erskine became a drifter. His family disowned him and he began an unsuccessful career as a small-time crook, ending up in jail ten times. His crimes included breaking open gas meters or stealing a few pounds from a purse left on a kitchen table. Sometimes he would steal bigger items – a TV set, an antique ornament, a camera, records, jewellery – which he would sell to backstreet dealers for a fraction of their worth. He tried to become a Rastafarian but other Rastafarians shunned him because of his habitual stealing.

With no permanent home, he lived in hostels and squats, or slept rough. So, even when the police knew that Erskine was the Stockwell Strangler, they would be hard pressed to find him. And time was of the essence as it was more than likely he would kill again.

Then they got lucky. The police discovered that Erskine was claiming unemployment benefit and he was due to pick up his next welfare cheque from the Social Security office in Southwark on 28 July. Plainclothes officers staked out the office and, when he joined the dole queue, they put the handcuffs on him. He did not struggle.

Although he was co-operative, detectives had trouble questioning Erskine as he had a low IQ with the reasoning ability of a ten-year-old. He spent much of the interrogation staring out of the window at the sky or giggling. The police were unable to discover where he had been living and his only possessions, apart from the clothes he stood up in, were a number of building society and bank books for the ten accounts he had opened to stash the proceeds of his burglaries. The total amounted to nearly £3,000. Tellingly, £350 had been paid in the day after William Carmen had been killed.

This was only circumstantial evidence. Clearly, it would be impossible to get a confession out of him. The palm print connected him to the murders of Janet Cockett and William Downes, and Fred Prentice picked him out at an identity parade in Clapham police station. However, Detective Chief Superintendent Thompson was keen to find evidence to link him to the other murders.

He took the unusual step of issuing a photograph to the media. A young businesswoman named Denise Keena came forward. The picture, she said, was that of a young man she had seen vomiting into the River Thames a couple of hundred yards from Florence Tisdall's flat on the evening she had been killed. She was just a few feet away when he turned and looked at her.

'He had this sort of terrible grin on his face,' she said. 'He looked as if he was out of control. It was a terrible, awful, disgusting expression. He had wide staring eyes and his mouth was open. All the muscles and tendons in his face were standing out, drawn tight against the bones.'

He appeared so manic that she had called the police, but by the time they arrived he had disappeared. After his arrest she picked him out in an identity parade and testified against him in court.

FAME AT LAST

Kenneth Erskine was charged with seven murders and one attempted murder. His trial began in the Old Bailey on 12 January 1988. He pleaded not guilty to all the charges, though he seemed unaware of what was going on and stared vacantly around the courtroom.

The prosecution said Erskine as a 'killer who liked killing'. Describing his assault on Fred Prentice, prosecutor James Crespi said: 'He jumped on Mr Prentice, putting one knee on each hand to immobilize him and his hands on his neck with the thumbs on his windpipe, pressing with a pumping action. He appeared to be playing with his victim.'

When Prentice himself took the witness stand, he told the court: 'I shouted at him to get out of my home. Then he was on top of me. I will never forget the cunning grin he had on his face as he tried to kill me.'

Detectives gave testimony concerning his motive from the questions they had asked him during his interrogation.

'What motive was there for me to murder?' he had said. 'I have done some burglaries in my time but I have never been violent.' Later he said: 'I thought I would never be caught.'

Asked: 'Do you want to be famous, is that it?' he replied: 'Yes, yes, I used to act a little.'

Evidence was presented that, in the case of two of the women and three of the men, the victims had been sodomized, but it was impossible to tell whether this had happened before or after death. In the case of Florence Tisdall, the killer had used enough pressure to break her neck.

Summing up after 18 days of evidence, Mr Justice Rose reminded the jury that the defendant had a mental age of 11 and a very poor memory. But this did not make him incapable of testifying on his own behalf in court.

'Those who are simple, and children of 11 and younger can and do give evidence in court,' he said.

Kenneth Erskine is taken into court with a detective on either side of him.

There was only one question the jurors had to consider: 'Did he do these things? That is something you must decide on the evidence, coolly, without emotion, unaffected by the horrific nature of some of the things you have heard.'

Erskine was convicted on all charges. Sentencing him to life, the judge said: 'The horrific nature and number of your crimes requires that I should recommend to the Secretary of State that you serve a minimum of 40 years.' It was then the longest minimum term for murder in the history of British crime. He added: 'I waste no further words in cataloguing the chilling horror of what you did.'

As Erskine was clearly mentally disturbed he was sent to the secure hospital at Broadmoor. There, on 23 February 1996, he prevented fellow inmate, convicted killer Paul Wilson, from strangling the Yorkshire Ripper Peter Sutcliffe with the flex from a pair of stereo headphones.

In 2004, Erskine was diagnosed with chronic schizophrenia and antisocial personality disorder. He had probably been suffering from the same conditions at the time of the murders. On appeal, his murder convictions were reduced to manslaughter on the grounds of diminished responsibility. He took little interest in the proceedings, falling asleep and, at one point, snoring.

CHAPTER TWENTY-THREE

ELMER WAYNE HENLEY

The Houston Mass Murder

AN ACCOMPLICE OF CANDY Man serial killer Dean Corll and his lover David Brooks, Elmer Wayne Henley joined in the slaughter of at least 28 teenage boys and young men in Houston, Texas, in the early 1970s. While he was convicted on six murder charges, he had brought the slaughter to an end by killing Corll and calling the police.

Born in Houston in 1956, Elmer Wayne Henley was the son of an alcoholic father who physically assaulted his wife and children. Nevertheless, he did well at school, until his parents divorced in 1970. He dropped out to take menial jobs to help support his mother and younger siblings. He also veered into crime, being arrested for assault in 1970 and burglary in 1972.

School friend and fellow truant David Brooks introduced him to Dean Corll, who picked out houses for them to burgle. It was, Corll said, a test. He was then asked if they were prepared to kill, if necessary. Henley said yes. Corll also said that he was part of a paedophile ring that was searching for young boys to take into sex slavery. He offered Henley $200 per recruit, the same amount he was paying Brooks.

Henley already knew that young boys were disappearing from the local Houston Heights neighbourhood. Eight had vanished in the past year. Two of them, 16-year-old David Hilligiest and 13-year-old Gregory

Malley Winkle, had been friends of his. On 29 May 1971, they had been on their way to a local swimming pool when they were seen getting into a white van, which later turned out to be Corll's. That evening Winkle had phoned his mother saying they had gone to Freeport, 95 km (60 miles) away, with some friends and would be home soon.

When they did not return, their families contacted the police, only to be told that the missing boys were runaways.

'You don't run away with nothing but a bathing suit and 80 cents,' said Gregory Winkle's mother.

Henley had visited the families, joined the search and volunteered to distribute the posters they had printed. Nevertheless, short of money, he agreed to abduct boys for Corll. What Henley did not know then was that Corll had raped, tortured and killed at least nine boys already, including Hilligiest and Winkle.

BECOMING A WILLING ACCOMPLICE

The first murder Henley seems to have been involved in was that of 17-year-old Willard 'Rusty' Branch, the son of a Houston police officer who died of a heart attack during the search. He had disappeared on 9 February 1972. His body was found under Corll's boatshed in south-west Houston in July 1985. He had been castrated before being shot dead.

The procedure of capturing boys was simple. Henley would invite any likely candidate back to Corll's place to drink or smoke marijuana. Henley would then show the victim a trick. He would handcuff himself behind his back, then he would invite the mark to do the same. This time, the cuffs would be locked. Corll would then pounce, put duct tape over the victim's mouth and tie his legs together. Henley was told that he would then be sold into sex slavery and, the following day, Henley would get his $200.

On 24 March 1972, Henley persuaded his 18-year-old friend Frank Aguirre to come back to Corll's house to smoke marijuana. However, once Aguirre was handcuffed, Corll dragged him into his bedroom and secured him to a makeshift torture board that had handcuffs and ropes at the corners. Henley claimed that he tried to talk Corll out of raping and killing Aguirre, but Corll told him that's what had happened to Branch and went ahead anyway. He later told Henley the same thing had happened to Hilligiest and Winkle, and it was too late to back out now.

On 20 April, Henley helped Corll abduct another friend, 17-year-old Mark Scott. He fought back furiously when Corll tried to secure him to the torture board, but gave up when Henley covered him with Corll's gun. He was raped, tortured and strangled, then, according to Henley, buried 95 km (60 miles) away at High Island Beach, though his body was never found.

On 26 June, Henley assisted Corll and Brooks in the abduction of 17-year-old Billy Baulch and 16-year-old Johnny Delone. According to Brooks, the youths were tied to Corll's bed and, after they were tortured and raped, Henley manually strangled Baulch, then shouted 'Hey, Johnny!' and shot Delone in the forehead, with the bullet exiting through the youth's ear. But this did not kill him. Delone then pleaded with Henley: 'Wayne, please don't!' Then he too was strangled.

The police also insisted that Baulch and Delone were runaways. Indeed, three days after they disappeared, the Baulches got a letter from Madisonville, Texas, saying: 'Dear Mom and Dad, I am sorry to do this, but Johnny and I found a better job working for a trucker loading and unloading from Houston to Washington and we'll be back in three to four weeks. After a week I will send money to help You and Mom out. Love, Billy.'

The address on the envelope was in Billy's handwriting but that of the letter itself was barely recognizable. What's more, Billy's father was a truck driver and knew that no such job existed. He suspected Corll, but when he confronted him Corll said he had no idea where the two boys had gone.

Seventeen-year-old Steven Sickman was last seen leaving a party in the Heights on 20 July. His body was recovered from Corll's boatshed in 1985. His ribs had been broken before he was strangled with a nylon cord. On 3 October, Henley helped abduct 14-year-old Wally Jay Simoneaux from outside his school and 13-year-old Richard Hembree, who was last seen alongside his friend in a white van parked outside a Heights grocery store. Simoneaux attempted to call his mother but was cut off. They were taken back to Corll's place for a party and given paint to sniff. When they had passed out, they were strapped to the torture rack and repeatedly raped. This went on for several days.

According to Brooks, Henley was waving Corll's .22 round when he accidentally shot Hembree in the jaw. The boys were later strangled and buried under Corll's boatshed.

Nineteen-year-old Richard Kepner was on the way to a pay phone to call his girlfriend when he was abducted. He was strangled and buried at High Island Beach. Brooks and Henley assisted in the interment of the bodies.

On 1 February 1973, Corll abducted and killed 17-year-old Joseph Lyles, who lived on the same street as Brooks, apparently without the assistance of Henley who was trying to join the US Navy at the time. However, he was rejected because he had no high-school diploma. He later admitted: 'I couldn't leave anyway. If I did go, I knew Dean would go after one of my little brothers, who he always liked a little too much.'

Henley's 15-year-old friend Billy Lawrence was abducted on 4 June. Henley had called his father and asked if Billy could go fishing with some friends. After three days' abuse and torture, Billy was strangled and buried at Lake Sam Rayburn.

Twenty-year-old Raymond Blackburn was hitchhiking from the Heights to see his newborn child on 15 June when he was picked up. He was strangled at Corll's home and buried at Lake Sam Rayburn.

Henley met 15-year-old Homer Garcia when they were both enrolled at a Bellaire driving school. Invited to a party at Corll's on 7 July, he was shot in the chest and head before being buried at Lake Sam Rayburn.

John Sellars was killed on 12 July, two days before his 18th birthday. He was shot in the chest and buried at High Island Beach, the only victim to be buried fully clothed. A week later 15-year-old Michael Baulch, Billy's younger brother, was strangled and buried at Lake Sam Rayburn, north-east of the city.

On 25 July, Henley lured two more friends, 17-year-old Charles Cobble and his flatmate, 18-year-old Marty Jones, to Corll's apartment where, two days later, Cobble was shot and Jones strangled before the youths were buried under Corll's boatshed.

The son of Seventh Day Adventists, 13-year-old James Dreymala was last seen riding his bike in south Houston on 3 August. He called his parents to tell them that he was at a party across town. He was strangled and buried at Corll's boatshed, seemingly without the assistance of Henley.

These helpless boys were subjected to such tortures as having their pubic hairs pulled out one by one, objects inserted into their anuses and glass tubes shoved into their penises, then broken. Some of their genitals had been chewed. Other victims had been castrated.

PUSHED TO BREAKING POINT

On 8 August 1973, Henley brought 19-year-old Timothy Kerley to Corll's. After drinking and sniffing paint the two teenagers went out to buy some sandwiches. On the way, Henley stopped by to see 15-year-old Rhonda Williams, who had been the girlfriend of Frank Aguirre. They had hoped to get married. That evening she had been beaten by her drunken father and was determined to leave home. Henley invited her to spend the night partying at Corll's home. When they turned up with Rhonda, Corll was furious, telling Henley that he had 'ruined everything' by bringing a girl.

After two hours drinking and smoking marijuana, Henley, Kerley and Williams passed out. Henley awoke to find Corll snapping handcuffs on to his wrists.

His ankles had already been bound together. Kerley and Williams were lying face-down on the floor beside Henley. They were bound with nylon rope and gagged with adhesive. Kerley had been stripped naked.

Corll told Henley that he was going to kill him along with the other two once he had finished raping and torturing Kerley. It was to be Henley's punishment for bringing a girl into the house. After kicking Williams repeatedly in the chest, he dragged Henley into the kitchen and poked his .22 into his stomach as if to kill him. Henley begged for his life and told Corll he would participate in the torture of Kerley and Williams, if he let him live.

Agreeing, Corll then untied Henley and took the handcuffs off. Kerley and Williams were then secured either side of the torture board – Kerley on his front, Williams on her back. Corll took off his clothes, then handed Henley his hunting knife and told him to cut off Williams' clothes. He was to rape her while Corll did the same to Kerley.

Williams then came round and whispered to Henley: 'Is this for real?

''Yes,' he said.

'Are you going to do anything about it?' she asked.

Under the circumstances Henley found that he could not get an erection. Corll teased him about it. Henley asked if he could take Rhonda into another room. When Corll ignored his request, Henley grabbed Corll's .22 and said: 'You've gone far enough, Dean.'

Corll turned towards Henley and advanced on him, taunting: 'Kill me, Wayne. You won't do it.'

Wayne Henley led police to the buried bodies of some 23 young boys killed in a three-year spree of sex and sadism.

Henley pulled the trigger, shooting Corll in the forehead. Corll continued advancing and Henley fired twice more, hitting him the shoulder. This spun him around. Then Henley unloaded another three shots into Henley's back as he staggered from the room. He fell dead.

Henley released the other two from the torture board and they dressed as best they could. He then called the police and told them that he had just killed a man. When officers turned up, they found the three teenagers sitting on the porch outside. After he was read his Miranda rights, Henley waived his right to silence, shouting: 'I don't care who knows about it. I have to get it off my chest!'

At the station, the police could hardly take in the story Henley told them. As well as admitting to killing Corll, he told them of the other murders. He then directed them to the boatshed where they began digging. Soon they found bodies wrapped in plastic sheets along with severed genitals in sealed bags. That evening, accompanied by his father, Brooks handed himself in. He denied any participation in the murders, but admitted that he knew Corll had raped and killed two youths in 1970.

Henley also accompanied the police to Lake Sam Rayburn to show them where more bodies were buried. Brooks continued to deny that he had had a hand in the murders, but admitted that he had been present at some of the killings and assisted in the burials. Then he and Henley accompanied the police to High Island Beach.

Henley was convicted of six murders and given six consecutive 99-year sentences – 594 years in all. Brooks was convicted of just one murder and was sentenced to a single term of 99 years. Henley was not charged with the slaying of Dean Corll. It was considered justifiable homicide. In jail, he took up painting and caused controversy when a Houston gallery hosted a show of his artwork.

CHAPTER TWENTY-FOUR

KENDALL FRANÇOIS

The Poughkeepsie Killer

POUGHKEEPSIE IS A SMALL city with a population of just 30,000 people 113 km (70 miles) up the Hudson River from New York. But in the 1990s it had a big city problem with drugs and prostitution. Then, in 1996, some of the streetwalkers began to go missing. Detective Lieutenant William Siegrist of the City of Poughkeepsie Police, who followed up on the missing persons reports, became convinced that a serial killer was at work. He contacted the FBI, but they could not help because, with no bodies, Siegrist could not even show that a crime had been committed.

'For two years, we were hunting a ghost,' said Siegrist. 'Nobody really knew what happened to these women. We had no crime scene, no bodies, no nothing – until the day we arrested François.'

The name of Kendall François had come up in the investigation, but Siegrist and his men could find no conclusive evidence against him. The disappearances had begun in October 1996, when 30-year-old Wendy Meyers was reported missing. She was described as a white female, with a slim build, hazel eyes and short brown hair, and was last seen at the Valley Rest Motel in Highland, a small town just across the river from Poughkeepsie where she was well known to the city police.

Then in December, 29-year-old Gina Barone was reported missing by her mother. Again, she was petite with brown hair. She had last been seen on 29 November having a row with a man on a street corner in Poughkeepsie. This was when Lieutenant Siegrist became interested. The two cases showed certain similarities. The two girls travelled in the same circles in the same city and both suddenly disappeared.

'It seemed like more than a coincidence,' he said.

Then in January 1997, 47-year-old Kathleen Hurley disappeared. She was last seen walking along Main Street in the downtown area of Poughkeepsie. Like the others, she was white, with brown hair and a small build.

A SUSPECT IS QUICKLY IDENTIFIED

During his enquiries Lieutenant Siegrist discovered that some of the Main Street prostitutes were complaining about a local man who was violent during sex. His name was Kendall François and he lived at 99 Fulton Street, which was in the town of Poughkeepsie, rather than the city. Siegrist contacted the police there who told him that a complaint had been made recently against François by a prostitute who claimed he had assaulted her.

Police kept an eye on François' house, but several weeks of surveillance produced no results. Then they fitted a prostitute with a wire. She engaged him in conversation several times, but no useful information was forthcoming.

On 7 March 1997, 31-year-old Catherine Marsh was reported missing by her mother. She had last been seen alive in the City of Poughkeepsie four months earlier on 11 November 1996. Like the other girls, she was white and petite, with brown hair. Clearly, she had not just moved on as her clothes and personal items were still in her apartment.

Twenty-seven-year-old Michelle Eason was reported missing on 9 October 1997. Last seen in the downtown area of Poughkeepsie, she was also petite – just 157 cm (5 ft 2 in) and weighing 52 kg (115 lb). Unlike the others, she was African-American.

Also in October, the mother of 29-year-old Mary Healy Giaccone died. Her father, a retired New York State corrections officer, contacted the City of Poughkeepsie Police, asking them to find Mary and tell her that her mother was dead. They soon discovered that the petite Mary had not been seen on the streets since February. On 13 November, the police themselves filed a missing persons report. And in December 1997, a headline in the *Poughkeepsie Journal* asked: 'Is There A Serial Killer On The Loose?'

In early January 1998, the police took in François for questioning. He was happy to talk and ostensibly co-operative, but two hours of interrogation yielded nothing. After the interview, the police accompanied him back to his house. Unlike the rest of the street, it was in a state of ill repair. The windows were filthy. Inside, the place was crammed with rubbish, soiled clothes and rotting food. The stench was awful. François' father slept on an oily sofa in the living room. His sister slept on a mattress on the floor in a back room littered with pornographic magazines, men's underwear, condom wrappers, rubber gloves and duct tape. Maggot casings rained down from the ceiling. François and his mother, a psychiatric nurse, slept upstairs. His room was stacked with pornographic videos.

Later that month François was arrested for assaulting prostitute Lora Gallagher. She said that he had taken her back to his house. They had a dispute about money and he punched her in the face, knocking her down on the bed. He got on top of her, put his hands around her throat and began choking her. She agreed to have sex with him. When he had finished he took her back to Cannon Street where he had picked her up.

She reported the incident and the police arrested him. On 5 May François pleaded guilty to third-degree assault and was sentenced to 15 days in jail, serving just seven. Four weeks later, on 12 June, 51-year-old Sandra French was reported missing from the small town of Dover, 32

Kendall François lived in a dilapidated house crammed with rubbish, soiled clothes and rotting food. Maggot casings rained down from the ceiling.

km (20 miles) east of Poughkeepsie. She was white, 152 cm (5 ft) and just 54 kg (120 lb). Her car was found just three blocks from François' home.

A COMMUNITY LIVING IN TERROR

The citizens of Poughkeepsie were becoming concerned. There was criticism that the police were not doing enough because the missing women were prostitutes, some of whom had a drug problem.

'We're low lifes, that's what it comes down to. People don't care that we're missing because they think we don't belong on the streets in the first place. It's not just the police, it's the community,' a prostitute told the *Poughkeepsie Journal*.

As it was the police could not even say that the cases were linked. Nevertheless, a task force was set up. It did not stop the disappearances. On 26 August 1998, 25-year-old Catina Newmaster vanished. Like the others, she was petite with brown hair and was last seen in the streets of downtown Poughkeepsie.

Then the police got lucky. City of Poughkeepsie Detective Skip Mannain and Town of Poughkeepsie Detective Bob McCready were in an unmarked car carrying flyers asking the public for help in the Catina Newmaster disappearance. They passed a large man in a white Toyota Camry and waved to him. It was Kendall François, who they knew from previous encounters.

They pulled into a petrol station. The attendant came over and told them that a woman who was walking away had said she had just been assaulted. They chased after her. Her name was Diane Franco. She was a prostitute and said that she had been taken to a house in Fulton Street for sex where the client had tried to strangle her. She knew the man who had attacked her. He was a regular and his name was Kendall François.

His huge hands had wrapped around her throat and his thumbs pressed into her flesh. Fearing for her life, she fought with all her might and, although she was just 59 kg (130 lb), managed to wriggle free. He had agreed to take her back to Main Street, but when he stopped in the petrol station she had jumped out of the car. The police took her to the station where she filed a complaint.

Two detectives went to pick up François. After being read his Miranda rights, he admitted that he had tried to choke Diane during sex. He made a formal confession, then asked to see the photographs of the missing prostitutes. He picked out four, saying: 'I killed them.' Of another three he said: 'I'm not sure about those.'

The following morning a team was sent to search the house at 99 Fulton Street. Over the next three days, eight bodies were removed. Five were found in the attic, three in a crawlspace in the basement. It seems that the smell of their rotting flesh was masked by the general stench in the house.

A BIG MAN BROUGHT LOW
Born in Poughkeepsie in 1971, François had been teased about his size as a child. At school he was successful on the football and wrestling teams. After graduating in 1989, he joined the US Army and was posted to Honolulu – where a spate of female strangulations from that time remains unsolved.

Discharged in 1994, he returned to Poughkeepsie when he found work with the education authority. The children called him 'stinky' behind his back. Girls in the red-light district also complained of his odour.

On 24 October 1996, he picked up Wendy Meyers. Back at his house, she insisted on being paid first. He strangled her and washed her body before putting it in a plastic back and stashing it in the attic. Two days later, her boyfriend reported her missing.

Gina Barone was only out on the streets on 11 November because she had had an argument with her boyfriend. After sex, François complained that he had been ripped off and grew angry and strangled her. They were in his car and he pushed her body down under the seat. He left it in the garage overnight. The following morning, he put it in a black bag and laid it next to Wendy's in the attic.

Two days later François killed Cathy Marsh. He squeezed her throat so hard that her hyoid bone snapped. The body was washed and placed next to the other two. They were joined by those of Kathleen Hurley and Mary Giaccone. Michelle Eason was never found.

He strangled Sandra French during sex, but the attic was getting a bit full, so he took her body down into the basement where he dug a shallow grave in the crawlspace and covered it with a thin layer of earth.

On 12 August, he took 34-year-old Audrey Pugliese down into the basement. She was not even on Lieutenant Siegrist's list as she had not been reported missing. During sex, François started punching her in the face. She managed to struggle out from under his huge bulk and made for the door. He caught up with her and continued punching her around the face and head. When she fell to the floor, he stamped his foot down on her face, her ribs and her stomach. She tried to get up but he grabbed her around the throat. When she was dead, he dumped her body on top of Sandra French's. Catina Newmaster joined them 13 days later.

The forensic team spent four weeks combing the house at 99 Fulton Street for evidence. On 13 October 1998, the grand jury handed down an indictment for eight counts of second-degree murder and upped the assault on Diane Franco to second degree. Knowing that the prosecution would be seeking the death penalty, François' attorney persuaded him to plead guilty on all counts so that he would only get life.

François was given 25 years on each count of murder to be served consecutively – 200 years in all – plus between one-and-a-half and three years for the assault on Diane Franco. He announced to the court that no other person had helped him commit the crimes, though there was speculation that his mother, who had psychiatric training, should have known that something was going on. His attorney also told the court that François was HIV positive, having been infected by one of his victims.

He was sent to Attica prison, where he was visited in 2008 by Catherine Marsh's mother Marguerite. She said she hoped to hear an apology from the killer, but never got one. But she said she forgave him. City of Poughkeepsie Police Chief Ron Knapp also visited him, but he continued to deny that he had killed Michelle Eason, a known drug user and prostitute.

'It's the one open case that we felt he may have had more knowledge on,' he said.

Of the Eason disappearance, Lieutenant Siegrist said: 'Although I believed that she was a part of this in the beginning, I don't believe it anymore. All the girls involved in the François case were white and were found inside François' home.'

There were no new leads and her disappearance remains a complete mystery.

François died of natural causes in the Wende Correctional Facility in Erie County, New York, on 11 September 2014, having served less than 16 years of his sentence. His house in Poughkeepsie still stands.

CHAPTER TWENTY-FIVE

LORENZO GILYARD

The Kansas City Strangler

LORENZO GILYARD'S MURDER SPREE lasted 16 years, from 1977 to 1993, and claimed the lives of at least 13 women, all but one prostitutes. His pattern of criminal behaviour went on much longer and he was only caught in 2004 thanks to the diligence of Kansas City Police Detective Mike Luster. Years after the last known murder, he was re-investigating the killings of two women that were linked by a common DNA sample. Over three years, he managed to link the DNA to ten other crime scenes, after which the crime lab got a match to a blood sample given by Gilyard in 1987.

Born in 1950, Lorenzo Gilyard came from a dysfunctional family. His father was convicted of assault and rape. His younger brother Darryl was sentenced to life without parole for a drug-related murder, while his sister Patricia, a sex worker, was convicted of the murder of a customer in a dispute over $35 and sentenced to ten years. She was also implicated in the murder of another hooker, but charges were dropped.

Gilyard's deviant behaviour began with his marriage to Rhena Hill in 1968. They divorced in 1973 after what she described as 'five years of torture'. They had met at high school and went dancing together. Then she fell pregnant. She said he was fun, but that changed once they were married. He continually abused her mentally and physically.

'He beat me and raped me,' she said. 'He threatened me and said he'd kill me.'

She had no freedom, even in her own home.

'He loves nice things, pretty things,' she said. 'But you can't use them. He made me live in one room, the bedroom, for five years.'

She complained that he had destroyed her life and sought psychiatric help for the abuse she suffered. But Gilyard's abuse was not confined to his wife. Just a year into the marriage he was accused of entering an acquaintance's home, hitting her on the head with a flashlight and raping her. She identified Gilyard as her assailant.

Two years later prosecutors filed rape charges against Gilyard. The complainant said that she knew her attacker, occasionally chatting to him on the street. She said he choked her with a headscarf and pantyhose. She fell unconscious. When she came to, her assailant said he was scared that she was going to report him to the police and began telling her about himself. Then he tried to scare her into silence. She picked his picture out of a photo lineup.

A 25-year-old stripper accused him of rape in February 1974. She identified Gilyard's Chevrolet convertible and picked him out of a lineup. He was arrested, but none of these accusations stuck. However, the following July he was charged with beating and raping the 13-year-old sister of a friend. He told police that she was lying. In the end, he pleaded guilty to molesting the girl and was sentenced to nine months in Jackson County Jail. When he got out, he began to murder.

TAKING UP A CAREER IN KILLING

His first three victims were wayward teenagers working as novice street prostitutes. They were killed in one place and their bodies dumped in another. Seventeen-year-old Stacie Swofford was killed on 17 April 1977 and dumped in a rubble-strewn lot. The body of 15-year-old Gwendolyn Kizine, his youngest victim, was left in an alley on 23 January 1980. A happy-go-lucky girl, she attended a holy-roller church before she got mixed up with a bad crowd, and turned to drugs which she paid for by prostitution. Then 17-year-old Margaret Miller was found in a vacant lot in May 1982.

Meanwhile, Gilyard had married for the third time – he had four wives in all and fathered 11 children. In 1979 he was accused of kidnapping a couple and raping the woman while holding her boyfriend at gunpoint. Although the boyfriend picked Gilyard out from a police lineup and hairs from the victim were found in the building where Gilyard was employed as a maintenance worker, a jury acquitted him of rape in September 1980.

That same year, he was convicted of aggravated assault for threatening to shoot his third wife. She divorced him in January 1981. The following month, Gilyard assaulted his ex-wife twice – beating and pistol-whipping her during one attack and breaking her front teeth and stabbing her in the arm with an ice pick in a second. He was convicted of third-degree assault in each case and was sentenced to probation.

In November 1981, Gilyard was sentenced to four years for burglary. However, he posted a $3,500 appeal bond and remained free for six months. During that time he killed 17-year-old Margaret Miller. A week after her body was found, Gilyard went to jail and the killings stopped.

He was released in January 1983, but soon returned to jail for violating his parole conditions by making a bomb threat. Freed in January 1986, he went to work for Deffenbaugh Disposal Services where his father worked. The killings began again. On 14 March the body of 34-year-old Catherine Barry was found under a pile of scrap plywood in a derelict building a few miles from downtown, her usual stamping ground. She was the only victim who was not a prostitute. A married mother of three, she had had a mental breakdown and ended up on the streets.

On 16 August, the body of 23-year-old Naomi Kelly was found. A single mother, she had been strangled and her body dumped in a downtown needle park. Then on Thanksgiving Day, 27 November, the body of 32-year-old Debbie Blevins, naked except for a pair of socks, was dumped outside a church.

Many of his victims were found naked. Their shoes were missing and detectives considered the possibility that a foot fetishist was at work. Most had been sexually assaulted. They had tell-tale scratches, cuts and broken fingernails, showing they had fought for their lives. All had been strangled. Six of them had ligatures around their necks – a shoelace, an electrical cord and items of their clothing, anything that was to hand. Many of the bodies were posed and several appeared to have been bound at the wrists.

On Good Friday, 36-year-old stripper Ann Barnes was found murdered. It was the tenth anniversary of the murder of Stacie Swofford, Gilyard's first victim. Seven weeks later, on 9 June, 20-year-old junkie and hooker Kellie Ann Ford was found murdered. The body of 19-year-old Angela Mayhew was found in North Kansas City on 12 September. Like others, she was shoeless. Hers was the only body that did not contain semen, though Gilyard's hair was found on her sweater.

Thirty-six-year-old Sheila Ingold was found dead in a van on Troost Avenue, a popular street for prostitutes, on 3 November. Thirty-year-old Carmeline Hibbs was found murdered on 19 December in a parking lot on Broadway a few blocks from where Ingold's corpse was left. She, too, was shoeless though it was a cold December night. A known user of prostitutes, Gilyard was one of a number of men asked to provide blood samples during the investigation of Ingold's death. He did so voluntarily. It was this that finally put him away.

ENJOYING A LIFE OF RETIREMENT
Gilyard then took a break of over five years. During that time, he worked his way up from being a rubbish collector on the back of the truck to a driver, then supervisor. Colleagues described him as reliable, friendly, helpful, hard-working and quick to make a joke.

'He had respect for his peers and was even-tempered and friendly,' a spokesman for the company said. 'He would bring gifts to people here regularly, like on their birthdays.'

People on his street described him as a 'real nice guy, a nice neighbour'. When collecting rubbish on his street, he knocked on the door of a neighbour who had forgotten to put their bin bags out.

He married for a fourth time. This marriage would last for a decade. On their front door, the couple hung a wooden sign with the name 'Gilyard' on it and 'Lorenzo' and 'Jackie' underneath. When a neighbour's daughter was selling Girl Scout cookies, he bought three boxes. Others remembered only seeing him when he was cleaning his car or chipping golf balls in the garden.

However, it was not all sweetness and light. In March 1989, after helping a neighbour load a bicycle into a car, he invited her to dinner. After a few glasses of wine, Gilyard reached across the table and began tugging at her top, saying he wanted to see her breasts. She backed away.

'I kept telling him that all I wanted to do was go home,' she said. 'Let me go home. Let me go home.'

Pinning her to the bed, he held a knife to his throat and threatened to kill himself. Then he held the knife to her throat. When he finally let her go, she called the police. He was charged with assault, sexual abuse and forcible sodomy. On a plea bargain, he pleaded guilty to everything but the sodomy charge and was given three years' probation and ordered to seek counselling. The complainant had agreed to the plea bargain because she did not want her mental health history to be discussed in open court.

The body of his final victim, 29-year-old Connie Luther, was found on 11 January 1993. Even though hers was the culmination of a series of murders, it rated less than 100 words on page six of the local news section of the *Kansas City Star*, the city's newspaper of record. The story read: 'The nude body of a Kansas City woman was found Monday on a sidewalk on the city's West Side. The woman, Connie Luther, 29, was found about 6:30 a.m. near 25th and Allen streets, investigators said. Police think she was killed elsewhere. A man who was driving to work Monday told police he discovered Luther's nude body face down in the snow among leaves and trash. Police have no suspects or motive. An autopsy will be performed to determine the cause of death.'

It is usually thought that serial killers do not stop unless they die or are put behind bars. But Gilyard did. That did not mean that there wasn't trouble. In September 1995, a neighbour complained that he had been stalking her. He would bring gifts of firewood or bottles of wine and make lewd remarks and gestures. He regaled her with intimate details of her body and it was plain that he had been peeping through her windows. She made it clear that she was not interested in him.

'I have pointed out to him that he is married, to which he simply shrugs and indicates that what his wife doesn't know won't hurt her,' she said.

It was clear that he wanted to control her.

'As a deaf single woman living alone,' she said, 'I fear for my safety and security in my house.'

In July 1996, she filed for a protection order, then moved out of town.

In 2001, another neighbour was moving a TV set into her house with her husband when they backed into Gilyard's driveway. Gilyard came out and pointed to a sign that read: 'Private Driveway. Do Not Enter.'

When the husband went inside Gilyard's house to discuss the matter, Gilyard showed him two guns. They reported the matter to the police.

Nevertheless, Gilyard managed to stay largely out of trouble until 2004, when the Kansas City Police Department received a federal grant to pay for lab time to test DNA evidence in cold cases. These matched DNA samples from the victims to the blood Gilyard had given in 1987.

Detective Mike Luster was said to be ecstatic when he heard a suspect was matched to the victims.

'We had put months and years into these investigations,' he said, adding that since the murders occurred, dozens of other detectives had put in a lot of work on the cases.

The police then put a tail on Gilyard and arrested him on 16 April in a Denny's restaurant in North Kansas City as he ate with a female co-worker. In a safe at his home, the police found shoes, bras and a pair of women's panties.

Gilyard was charged with seven first-degree murders and convicted of six – those of Catherine Barry, Naomi Kelly, Ann Barnes, Kellie Ford, Sheila Ingold and Carmeline Hibbs. He was acquitted of the murder of Angela Mayhew due to insufficient evidence.

'This is a victory for DNA testing,' Jackson County Prosecutor Mike Sanders said. 'It's another example of what DNA can do for us in law enforcement.'

Prosecutors said they would not seek the death penalty if Gilyard agreed to face a trial before a judge without a jury.

'He's forfeited any right to live here among the rest of us,' Judge John O'Malley said. 'That's the comfort we can derive.'

The judge added that there was a chance the women, most of whom were prostitutes, would have turned their lives around, 'except he stole everything from them'.

Gilyard was given six life sentences without possibility of parole. Behind bars in the Western Missouri Correctional Center, he continued to protest his innocence. No one believed him.

'I'd like to think that the citizens of Jackson County can sleep a little safer tonight knowing the person who is responsible for these deaths and murders is behind bars, and will be for the rest of his life,' prosecutor Jim Kanatzar said.

He said his office would be reviewing six other cases dismissed earlier to determine whether to refile them.

OTTIS TOOLE

The Jacksonville Cannibal

A SERIAL KILLER IN his own right, Ottis Toole went on a killing spree across America with the notorious mass murderer Henry Lee Lucas. Both made numerous confessions and recanted. Both were convicted of multiple murders. Both died in jail.

Like many serial killers, Toole was the son of an alcoholic father, as was Lucas. Both their mothers dressed them as girls when they were young. Lucas was the older of the two, born in 1936 in the backwoods of Virginia. Toole was born in 1947 in Jacksonville, Florida. While his mother was a religious fanatic, he claimed his grandmother was a Satanist. He said he watched her digging up body parts to use in her rituals.

With an IQ just above mentally retarded, Toole dropped out of school in the eighth grade. He'd supposedly been introduced to sex before the age of ten by his older sister and a gay neighbour, or possibly, he claimed, with a friend of his father's when he was five. Later he dressed in drag to pick up men. However, when a travelling salesman took him into some woods for sex when he was 14, he murdered the man by running him over with his own car.

His first arrest, for loitering, was in August 1964. Soon his rap sheet filled up with counts of petty theft and lewd behaviour. He married briefly, but his wife left him after three days because of his homosexuality. By 1974, Toole was drifting and touring the western states in an old

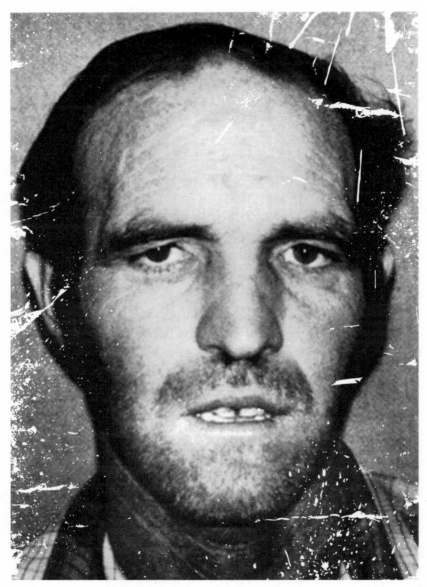

Ottis Toole used to dress in drag to pick up men. However, when a travelling salesman took him into some woods for sex when he was 14, he murdered the man by running him over with his own car.

pickup truck. On the way, he was thought to have murdered four more people before he met up with Lucas in a soup kitchen in Jacksonville in 1978. By then, Lucas had killed his mother and served five years for kidnapping three schoolgirls.

The pair 'joined forces as a homosexual crime team, criss-crossing the country from 1978–1983', according to John Walsh, the host of the TV show *America's Most Wanted* and the father of six-year-old Adam Walsh, who Toole admitted to murdering in 1983, though he later recanted. Although vital evidence, including Toole's impounded car and a machete, went missing, police in Hollywood, Florida announced in 2008 that they were convinced that Toole had murdered Adam Walsh and closed the case. The child disappeared from a mall in Hollywood in July 1981. His body was never found, but two fishermen found the boy's head in a canal two weeks after his disappearance.

In 1983, Toole was in Duval County Jail where he was being questioned about the murder of a woman near Lake Charles, Louisiana, the previous year. Twenty-year-old Catherine Martin had been stabbed 16 times with a screwdriver. While being interrogated, Toole said he had killed Adam Walsh too. He said that he had picked up the boy in the parking lot of the Sears' mall by offering him sweets and toys, but when they drove off, Adam said he wanted to go home and started crying.

'It was like the kid wouldn't shut up. I was driving him in the car. I slapped him. I hit him several times,' Toole said.

They stopped in the countryside, where Toole decapitated the child with a machete. After dumping the body, he drove around with the head for several days before chucking it in a canal. The police found blood soaked into the carpet of the car, but, without a body, it was impossible to make the charges stick.

In 1984, he admitted killing 18-year-old David Schallart, a hitchhiker he had picked up near Pensacola. His body was found in February 1980 off Interstate 10. There were five bullets in his head. He also confessed to the murder of 20-year-old Ada Johnson after kidnapping her at gunpoint from a Tallahassee nightclub in 1983. Again, she had five bullets in her head when her body was found outside Fort Walton Beach in Florida. He was found guilty and sentenced to death.

He was also convicted of murdering 64-year-old George Sonnenberg by locking him in his home and setting it alight. Toole got aroused at the sight of flames. He was sentenced to death for this murder too. But on appeal, both sentences were commuted to life. His other confessions brought him four more life sentences. In jail, Toole got to know Ted Bundy when they briefly lived in next-door cells in Raiford Prison in Florida.

Toole also claimed to have committed over 100 murders with Lucas, many of them for a mysterious cult called 'The Hand of Death', who paid them handsomely. In an interview with crime reporter Billy Bob Barton in Florida State Prison, Toole said he had killed numerous children and young people including 24-year-old Shelley Robertson, who disappeared on 30 June 1970, whose murder was formerly attributed to Ted Bundy. Her naked, decomposed body was found in a mine in Colorado in July 1975.

'I got her when she was hitchhiking in Colorado,' he said. 'I had me an old pickup truck. I picked her up, took her up into the Rocky Mountains and killed her. She was naked when I killed her. A pretty one. It was the summertime in 1974 and what was funny is that the police blamed the killing on Ted Bundy but Ted didn't get that one. I got her.'

He also admitted the murder of Sun Ok Cousin. Late on the night of 19 September 1974 a man entered Suezy's Oriental Massage Parlor in Colorado Springs, pulled a gun and demanded money from proprietor Sun Ok Cousin and masseuse Yon Cha Lee. The women surrendered $60 but that did not satisfy the intruder. He tied up Lee, stabbed her and sliced her throat, nearly killing her. In another room he raped Cousin and shot and stabbed her to death. Before fleeing he set both women on fire. Lee nevertheless survived.

Park Estep, a Vietnam veteran who had never been in trouble with the law, was charged with murder, robbery, assault, arson and rape and convicted only on Lee's identification, even though she continued to insist that her attacker had been clean shaven while Estep had a moustache. This alibi was also confirmed by his wife, who passed a lie-detector test.

In 1984 Toole told two private investigators who had formerly been deputies in El Paso County Sheriff's office in Colorado: 'You guys want me to tell you about when I went to the steam bath in Colorado.... Y'all found the lady lying on the front floor with the hell shot out of her.'

Estep had served ten years in jail, but the Colorado prosecutor Bob Russel insisted that Toole's confession was 'tainted'. He flew to Florida with an aide to interview Toole.

'We set out from the beginning to prove that the Toole confession was false,' he said. 'I don't want this killer Estep back on the street.'

After 85 minutes of cross-examination, Toole said: 'Okay. If you said I didn't kill her, then maybe I didn't.'

Returning to Colorado, Russel announced that Toole had recanted. Russel was running for office at the time.

'Can you believe this is happening to me just before my election?' he said. 'I'm going to lose votes if people think I have convicted an innocent man.'

Toole continued to insist that he killed Cousin. In 1996, he told Barton: 'Yeah. I got me a Chinese girl out by Colorado Springs in 1974; cut her throat and she had a friend and I stabbed her up, too. The cops got a guy named Estep for that case but I did it. Cops don't always get the right person.'

HUMAN SACRIFICES

Toole said that with children, both boys and girls, he would gag them so they couldn't scream, then sodomize them.

'After the f***ing then you strip them naked and hang them upside down by the ankles; then slit their throat with a knife, slit the belly and take out the guts, the liver, the heart. Cut off the head. Let the blood drain,' he said. Then he would make a barbecue pit. 'Charcoal so there ain't much smoke. Take down the body, put the metal spit through them. Put it into the asshole, through the body and out the neck, wire the meat to the spit, put it on the spit-holder over the coals. Damn tasty.'

He said they tasted like roasted piglets. Boys and girls tasted much the same up to ten years old. When they were teenagers, boys were gamier than girls. He said he preferred eating them when they were 14 years old, with a spicy sauce. He also claimed to have killed a pair of lovers he found in the woods, roasted them and ate their ribs.

He did this with Lucas too. They would pick up hitchhikers.

'We killed over 200 when we was roaming the country together,' he said. 'Maybe he killed more before he met me or after we split. I'd say around 200 for sure, I got over 100 my own self. Henry said he got about 400 altogether, I don't know for sure. I really don't.'

They joined The Hand of Death in the early 1980s.

'We were working for that cult and we'd grab little kids for the human sacrifices, grab young women for the snuff movies,' he told Barton. 'We'd tie the women up and haul them to Mexico.'

He said he liked working for The Hand of Death.

'They'd let me have the corpses when they were done with the films or sacrifices and I could take a prime cut,' he said.

The human sacrifices were part of a secret ritual. Teenaged virgin girls would be put on an altar and have their throats cut while burnt offerings were made to the devil. Blood would be collected in a goblet and drunk while it was still warm to the accompaniment of occult chants.

'It's secret stuff,' he said. 'You aren't supposed to reveal it. They make you take an oath for secrecy.'

The blood tasted salty. He didn't like it, he said, and preferred the cooked meat of humans.

During the rituals, cult members would eat the sexual parts of the child sacrifice. From girls, they would slice off the nipples and cut out the vagina. With boys, they would cut off the penis and testicles, putting the severed pieces in a stew pot.

'The guy who cooks it makes it like a soup or stew. It's a secret recipe from about 1,000 years ago.'

Asked if it tasted good, he said: 'Not bad. The part of the woman around the pussy hole is like lips. Sort of chewy and rubbery. The balls are damned good when fried. Use a little batter and a fryer and it's a real treat. Crispy. Like a crispy chestnut. Fresh fried balls is one of my favourites.'

Eating the sexual parts of their sacrifices was said to increase sexual potency, but Toole remained unconvinced.

'I prefer to eat the ribs actually but I go along with what's being served at the ceremonies,' he said.

Most of the victims were snatched in Texas and the sacrifices took place at a ranch in Mexico. The priests there usually wanted virgins for human sacrifice at certain times of the year.

'They'd say to me and Henry to go up to Texas and collect some,' Toole said. 'We'd drive on up, get girls hitchhiking... there are a lot of women just walking down the road in South Texas. Migrant workers. We'd get them, tie them up, gag them, put them in the trunk. We fill the trunk, six or eight girls, then go back to Mexico. Down at the ranch the priests check them for virgins.'

They would examine the girls' vaginas.

'The hole is smaller on virgins. Something about that hole, I'm not into women,' Toole said. 'The priests took the virgins to one building and the non-virgins went to where they made snuff films.'

He had watched a snuff movie being made where a woman was guillotined. Sometimes as many as 13 virgins would be sacrificed during a night by a priest dressed as a goat who raped them at the same time. Toole said that Lucas denied that this went on because he didn't want to face the death penalty, while his own death sentences had already been commuted.

'Henry is going to be executed but I'll be alive surrounded by cute f•••-boys,' he said. 'I have everything I want in prison. Except I miss the freedom to drive down the highway robbing and killing from town to town. That's excitement at its best and [I] miss being able to barbecue a boy when I get the urge.' Following this, he offered to supply Barton's readers with his recipe for barbecue sauce.

Ottis Toole died of cirrhosis of the liver in Florida State Prison, aged 49, on 15 September 1996. His body was unclaimed. Lucas died of heart failure aged 64, in prison on 12 March 2001. His grave is unmarked.

Chapter Twenty-seven

GENENE JONES

The Death Nurse

THERE ARE 'ANGELS OF Death' – nurses who work with old people and kill them as they approach the end of their lives. Then there are 'Death Nurses' who kill babies and young children who have hardly started theirs. Genene Jones fell into the second category, killing maybe as many as 50 infants.

Born in Texas in 1950, she was immediately given up for adoption. Her new parents, Gladys and Dick Jones, had three other adopted children, two older than Genene, one younger. They lived in a comfortable four-bedroom house in the suburbs of San Antonio. Her adoptive father Dick ran a nightclub until, when Genene was ten, he was arrested. A safe had been stolen from the house of a man who was in Jones' nightclub at the time of the burglary. When the safe turned up, Jones was suspected. He confessed, but claimed that the theft was a practical joke and charges were dropped. The nightclub then foundered. He opened a restaurant which also failed. Then he took to erecting billboards.

Through the resulting family tribulations, Genene felt overlooked and began calling herself the 'black sheep' of the family. To get attention, she feigned illness. At school she was shunned for being aggressive and manipulative. She was also short and overweight, which did not help.

Her closest companion was her younger brother Travis, two years her junior. When he was 14, he was making a pipe bomb that blew up in his face and killed him. A traumatized Genene screamed and fainted at the funeral.

A year later, her adoptive father died of cancer and her mother took to drink. To escape the family tragedies, Genene sought to marry. Underage, her mother would not allow it. Eventually, when she graduated, she married a high-school dropout who, after seven months, enlisted in the US Navy. She then began a series of affairs with married men. The couple divorced after four years while her husband was in hospital after an accident. The divorce papers indicate that it had been a violent relationship.

NO LOVE LIKE A MOTHER'S LOVE

Claiming that she had always wanted children, Genene Jones had two, but left them to be brought up by her mother, while she enrolled at beauty school. Fearing that hair dyes might give her cancer, Jones changed course. Having a penchant for medicine and doctors, she trained to become a Licensed Vocational Nurse, or LVN.

Her first job at San Antonio's Methodist Hospital lasted just six months. She was fired for making decisions that she was not qualified to take. Another job lasted little longer. Then she was hired by Bexar County Medical Center Hospital to work in their paediatric unit.

The first child she took care of had a fatal intestinal condition. When he died shortly after surgery, Jones broke down. She brought a stool into the cubicle where the body lay and sat staring at it. The other nurses could barely understand this. She hadn't known the child long and her grief seemed excessive.

Needing to be needed, she took care of the sickest children on the long 3–11 pm shift. It soon became known as the 'Death Shift'. Jones skipped classes on the proper handling of drugs and, in her first year, made eight elementary nursing errors, some concerning the dispensing of medication. Never liking to admit mistakes, she was bossy, telling other nurses what to do.

Foul-mouthed and always bragging about her sexual conquests, Jones was disliked by colleagues who regularly applied for transfers to get away from her. However, the head nurse Pat Belko protected her, even when she turned up for work drunk. She also upset new nurses by predicting which babies were going to die.

'Tonight's the night,' she would say. In one week, seven children died, often from conditions that should not have been fatal. Jones took a special interest in children that were near death and liked to be there when it happened, taking special pleasure informing and commiserating with the parents.

There were also numerous cases of children slipping into critical conditions in her care, then reviving during dramatic medical interventions. One child had a seizure three days in a row, but only on Jones' shift.

'They're going to start thinking I'm the Death Nurse,' Jones quipped.

Others thought so too, but Pat Belko sought to quash rumours that she was doing something to the children. This was just spiteful tittle-tattle from jealous colleagues, she maintained.

When Dr James Robotham became medical director of the paediatric unit, he took a more hands-on approach, leaving less for junior nurses to do. However, Jones ingratiated herself and basked in the attention he gave her.

She also sought attention by her old ruse of feigning illness, referring herself to the outpatients' unit 30 times in two years. This behaviour is now recognized as Munchausen syndrome.

Then, a six-month-old baby named Jose Antonio Flores went into cardiac arrest while in Jones' care. He was revived, but went into arrest again the next day during her shift and died from internal bleeding.

Tests on the corpse indicated an overdose of a drug called heparin, an anticoagulant. No one had prescribed it.

At the news of his son's death, the child's father had a heart attack. After helping the father to the emergency room, Jones seized the dead baby and made off down the corridor with the family in pursuit. She gave them the slip and delivered the dead child to the morgue. Nobody could explain this bizarre behaviour.

Being treated for pneumonia, Rolando Santos began having seizures, cardiac arrest, and extensive unexplained bleeding. This started, then intensified on Jones' shift. In a coma, blood came up into his throat and his blood pressure dropped dangerously. But after he was removed from the paediatric ICU and put under 24-hour surveillance, he survived.

Another child was sent to the paediatric unit to recover from open-heart surgery. Although he progressed well at first, on Jones' shift his condition deteriorated and he soon died. Jones grabbed a syringe and squirted fluid over the child in the sign of a cross, then did the same again on herself. Grabbing the dead baby, Jones began to cry.

Two resident physicians treating a three-month-old boy named Albert Garza suspected that Genene had probably given him an overdose of heparin. When they confronted her, she got angry, but after their intervention the child recovered. Following this incident tighter control was applied to the use of heparin, making nurses more accountable.

While Genene's health was deteriorating, at least according to her own account, she refused to take the drugs she had been prescribed. Again, she seemed to be angling for attention. Her former ally Dr Robotham began to express concerns about Jones. However, in November 1981, the hospital administration had a meeting and decided that Robotham was over-reacting. They were not willing to invite the attention a formal investigation would garner. Nevertheless, Dr

Robotham continued to keep an eye on the records of drug use on the 3–11 pm shift.

While the use of heparin was being monitored, 11-month-old Joshua Sawyer, who suffered a cardiac arrest after inhaling smoke during a fire at his home, was prescribed Dilantin, an anticonvulsant. While the doctors expected him to recover, Jones told his parents that it would be better to let him die as he would be suffering from brain damage. Suddenly, he had two more heart attacks and died. Tests showing a lethal dose of Dilantin in his blood were overlooked.

Finally, a committee was formed to look into the high mortality rate headed by Dr Robotham and Pat Belko. They decided not to put the blame on one nurse but to replace the LVNs on the unit with registered nurses, or RNs. That meant Jones would be transferred away from the paediatric unit. She promptly resigned.

A NEW LIFE IN A NEW TOWN, BUT THE DEATHS CONTINUE

In 1982, Dr Kathleen Holland opened a paediatric clinic in Kerrville, Texas. She hired Genene Jones, believing that she had been the victim of the male medical establishment at Bexar. Dr Holland had testified on Jones' behalf in the investigation and helped her move to Kerrville. However, she found she had bought into trouble. Children at the clinic began having seizures. In two months seven had to be transferred by ambulance to Kerr County's Sid Peterson Hospital, where the staff grew suspicious. In one case Jones was seen to inject something into the child. However, all recovered.

The first suspicious seizure happened on 17 September 1982, the very day the clinic first opened. The child was Chelsea McClellan, who had been born prematurely and was suffering from breathing problems. She was the clinic's first-ever patient. She had stopped breathing while in Jones' care, but she had placed an oxygen mask over the baby's face and they rushed her to an emergency room at the nearby Sid Peterson Hospital. To everyone's relief, the child recovered and Jones was showered with praise.

Nine months later, Chelsea returned to the clinic for a routine check-up and to have two inoculations. When Jones gave her the first, the child began having breathing difficulties. She had a seizure and her mother asked Jones to stop, but she went ahead and gave Chelsea the second injection anyway. She stopped breathing and was rushed to the Sid Peterson Hospital, but died in the ambulance on the way.

Jones allegedly said: 'And they said there wouldn't be any excitement when we came to Kerrville.'

She sobbed over the child's body and lovingly wrapped it in a blanket before presenting it to the parents. The cause of death was given as SIDS – sudden infant death syndrome, or cot death.

A week after the funeral, Chelsea's grief-wracked mother Petti visited her daughter's burial site to find Jones kneeling at the foot of the grave, sobbing and wailing the child's name over and over as if Chelsea had been her own.

'What are you doing here?' asked Petti.

Jones stared at her blankly, as if in a trance, and walked away without a word. When she was gone, Petti McClellan noticed that Jones had left a small token of flowers, but had also taken a bow from Chelsea's grave.

Meanwhile, a committee had been formed at the Sid Peterson Hospital to investigate the deaths. They asked Dr Holland if she used succinylcholine, a powerful muscle relaxant. She said she kept some in her office but did not use it. The committee notified the Texas Rangers.

Jones then claimed that she had taken an overdose of doxepin, a drug used to fight anxiety, and had her stomach pumped. In fact, she had taken just four tablets, faking a coma, and was in no danger. Then a bottle of succinylcholine went missing and Dr Holland fired Jones.

CAPTURED, BUT NO REST FOR HER VICTIMS' FAMILIES – YET

On 12 October 1982, a grand jury in Kerr County investigated the death of Chelsea McClellan and the eight other children from Dr Holland's clinic who had developed emergency respiratory problems. Chelsea's body was exhumed and succinylcholine was found in the tissue. Her death had been caused by an injection of the muscle relaxant.

In February 1983, another grand jury was convened in San Antonio to look into the 47 suspicious deaths of children at the Bexar County Medical Center Hospital that had occurred while Genene Jones had been there. Chelsea's parents began a lawsuit against Jones and Holland, alleging wrongful death. Meanwhile, Jones married a 19-year-old boy, seemingly to deflect rumours that she was a lesbian.

The Kerr County grand jury indicted Jones on one count of murder and several charges of injury to seven other children who had been injected with muscle relaxants. Then the San Antonio grand jury indicted her for injuring Rolando Santos by deliberately injecting heparin. She remained a suspect in ten infant deaths at the hospital.

There were two separate trials. The prosecution alleged that the motive was Munchausen syndrome by proxy – a psychological disorder where a caregiver indulges in attention-seeking behaviour by manipulating the health of their patients. Jones liked the excitement and the attention the sick children brought her. The children were at her mercy. They couldn't tell on her, so she was free to create the situation over and over again. There was no doubt that, over time, her actions had escalated and that she had taken more risks.

The first jury took just three hours to find Jones guilty of murdering Chelsea McClellan. She was given the maximum sentence of 99 years. Later, she was given another 60 years for injuring Rolando Santos. She had the possibility of parole, but the McClellans fought to keep her inside.

Genene Jones at a pre-trial hearing in 1984 – she was convicted of killing one infant, Chelsea McClellan, and nearly killing another, Rolando Santos, earning her a total of 159 years in prison.

However, she was due for mandatory release in 2018 to avoid prison overcrowding. To prevent this, fresh charges were brought for the murder of Joshua Sawyer. The Bexar County District Attorney said that more murder charges would be levelled against her to prevent her release. In September 2019, the San Antonio 399th State District Court set a 2020 date for Jones to stand trial for more charges of murder.

Chapter Twenty-eight

PATRICK KEARNEY

The Trash Bag Killer

PREYING ON YOUNG MEN in California from 1965 to 1977, Patrick Wayne Kearney was first known as the Freeway Killer. But as there were two other Freeway Killers – Randy Kraft and William Bonin – operating at around the same time, he came to be distinguished by the trademark method by which he dumped the dismembered bodies of his victims in trash bags.

Kearney had got away with murder for years until 17-year-old John LaMay went missing. On the evening of 13 March 1977, LaMay told his next-door neighbour that he going to see a guy called Dave he had met in a gym in downtown Los Angeles. He was gay and, since same-sex sexual intercourse had been decriminalized the previous year, many gay people had flocked to the Golden State.

When LaMay did not come home the following day, his mother called the El Segundo police. As usual in such cases, the police marked him down as another teenage runaway. But five days later his remains were found beside a highway near Corona. His body had been skilfully dismembered, drained of blood and washed. Then the parts had been packed into industrial trash bags and sealed with nylon filament tape. The head was missing, but a birthmark identified the remains as those of John LaMay.

'Dave' was identified as David Hill. Friends of LaMay supplied an address for him. He lived in an apartment owned by Patrick Kearney in Redondo Beach near Los Angeles.

The eldest of three sons, Kearney had been born in East Los Angeles. A thin and sickly child, he had been bullied at school. From the age of eight, he was fantasizing about killing people. When he was 13, his father taught him how to kill pigs by shooting them behind the left ear. He later used this technique to slaughter animals unsupervised and found pleasure in rolling around in the blood and guts.

He lived in Texas for a while, joining the US Air Force briefly there and having a short marriage. Then he moved back to California where, with a near genius IQ of 180, he went to work as an engineer at the Hughes Aircraft Company.

KILLING AS AN ACT OF REVENGE

While in Texas in 1962, Kearney met David Douglas Hill, a younger man from Lubbock. They became lovers. Hill had served in the army, but was discharged after being diagnosed with a personality disorder. Returning to Lubbock, he married his high-school sweetheart. This marriage too was short-lived. After meeting Kearney, he divorced and moved to California in 1967. They lived together, eventually moving to Redondo Beach.

Kearney went out to work while Hill kept house. But their relationship was tempestuous. Hill would frequently walk out and stay with friends, or have a one-night stand. Sometimes he would flee to Lubbock, but somehow they always got back together. While Hill was gone, Kearney would be seized with a murderous rage. He too would go out for sex.

Kearney would cruise gay bars or pick up hitchhikers in his Volkswagen. At just 165 cm (5 ft 5 in) and with a slight built, he liked bigger men, blond and arrogant, like those who had bullied him as a child. And he had a foolproof way of subduing them. Out on the open road, he would suddenly pull out a .22 pistol and shoot his victim in the head while keeping one hand on the steering wheel.

Alone with the body, he would undress it and sodomize the corpse. Sometimes he would take revenge for his childhood bullying by beating the dead and violated body. Then he would cut it up with a hacksaw, cleaning up thoroughly afterwards. Inspired by reading up on Dean Corll, he put the body parts in trash bags and dumped them beside the freeway.

With other Freeway Killers on the loose, the police were confused, but eventually began to recognize Kearney's distinctive signature. While Bonin and Kraft tortured their victims before strangling or stabbing them, Kearney always shot his man then dumped the remains in trash bags. The cops began to call his the 'fag in a bag' murders.

With an address for 'Dave', the police visited Kearney's home and interviewed Kearney and Hill, who appeared unperturbed. The detectives helped themselves to a few carpet fibres. For once, Kearney had been careless. A few carpet strands had got stuck to the tape he had used to seal the bags in which he had put LaMay. The fibres matched. Building a case, the police returned to get samples of pubic hair from Kearney and Hill, as well as some hairs from their dog. Thus alerted, Kearney destroyed the cuttings he had kept from the coverage of Dean Corll.

When the police visited a third time, they found that the couple had gone. But they had left behind a hacksaw with traces of blood and tissue. There was blood residue invisible to the naked eye in the bathroom, too. A search of Kearney's office at Hughes Aircraft found the same trash bags and nylon filament tape as the killer used. Posters were printed with Kearney and Hill's pictures on them.

Kearney and Hill had fled to El Paso, Texas. But with their photographs circulating, it was clear that they could not escape. They returned to California and at 1.30 pm on 1 July 1977 they walked into Riverside County Sheriff's office. They indicated the wanted poster on the wall with their pictures on it.

'That's us,' they said.

They were arraigned on two murders and the bail was set at $500,000 each. Questioned about six other murders, Kearney co-operated fully with the police. They asked him about picking up Marines, plying them with booze and pills, castrating them and leaving things jammed into their anuses – the signature of Randy Kraft.

'I am not the Wooden Stake,' he said.

He did not torture, strangle or stab, he said. He killed cleanly with a bullet to the head.

A LONG LITANY OF DEATH AND DISMEMBERMENT

The investigation into the Trash Bag Murders had been going on since 13 April 1975, when the body of 21-year-old Albert Rivera had been found in a heavy-duty trash bag near Highway 74, east of San Juan Capistrano. However, Kearney admitted committing his first murder in the spring of 1962. He did not know the victim's name, only that he was 19 and white. The boy had been persuaded to take a ride with him on his motorcycle. In a secluded spot near Indio, California, Kearney shot him and had sex with his dead body, then mutilated it. He did not know if it had ever been found. He also killed the boy's 16-year-old cousin who had seen them ride away together, along with another unknown victim, an 18-year-old named Mike.

The first murder on the charge sheet, though, was of a man known only as George. It happened at Christmas 1978, after Hill had moved into Kearney's apartment in Culver City. They had been visiting a friend of Hill's in Tijuana. Kearney had shot the man between the eyes while he was sleeping, then sodomized his dead body in the bathroom. While dismembering the corpse he also took the precaution of removing the bullet. The body was then buried behind his garage. When Kearney took the police there they dug up a body and found it had a single bullet hole in its skull – and no bullet.

Kearney did not kill again for over a year, fearing that the police would be investigating George's disappearance. But no one came knocking on his door. As he had seemingly got away with murder, he began his killing spree in earnest.

On 26 June 1971, he killed 13-year-old hitchhiker John Demichik. Then came 17-year-old James Barwick, another hitchhiker. Both bodies were found in 1973. The following year five-year-old Ronald Dean Smith Jr was killed. Albert Rivera, a homosexual prostitute, was next. After being shot in the head, he had been taken back to Kearney's house, sodomized, cut up and stuffed in trash bags. Later, in 1975, 20-year-old Larry Gene Walters, a hitchhiker, was shot at Kearney's house, sodomized, then dismembered and put into trash bags to be dumped in various locations.

Kenneth E. Buchanan was killed on 1 March 1976. Kearney shot him in the back of the head. But after he had sodomized him, he found that the 17-year-old loner was not dead. He came round, so Kearney shot him another three times. Three weeks later, Kearney picked up 13-year-old hitchhiker Oliver Peter Molitor and played 'doctor' with him to lure him into sex. He then killed the boy, cut him up and buried the pieces in several places at the Palos Verdes landfill.

Fifteen-year-old Larry Armedariz was killed on 19 April 1976. His body was never found. Neither was that of 13-year-old Michael Craig McGhee, who was killed on 11 June 1976. Kearney said he had picked up McGhee when he was hitchhiking from Inglewood Avenue near Lennox to Torrance. He befriended the boy and invited him on a camping trip to Lake Elsinore that weekend.

'I disposed of the body... You aren't going to find him,' Kearney told the police.

The body of 23-year-old John 'Woody' Woods was found a year after he was killed on 20 June 1976. The body of 17-year-old Larry Epsy was found that August. Later that month 20-year-old Wilfred Lawrence

Faherty was killed. His body was found the same day. Also in August 1976, 20-year-old hitchhiker Randall 'Randy' Lawrence Moore was killed. Twenty-year-old hitchhiker Mark Andrew Orach was shot in the head on 6 October 1976.

In the autumn of 1976, 17-year-old Robert 'Billy' Benniefiel accepted a lift from Kearney when his bicycle broke down. He was shot in the back of the head. Kearney then took his body back to his house and sodomized him, dismembered him and dumped his body parts in several different locations. It was never found. Also that autumn, 27-year-old soldier David Allen was shot in the head and left at the side of the road.

In November 1976, 19-year-old hitchhiker Timothy B. Ingham was picked up on the eastbound carriageway of Highway 79 near Indio and killed. His remains were thrown down a ravine and his personal possessions were given to friends of Kearney's in Mexico.

On 23 January 1977, 28-year-old prostitute Nicholas 'Nicky' Hernandez-Jimenez was killed and dismembered. Then in February 1977 Arturo Romos Marquez was shot and dismembered. His body was only found after Kearney confessed. Finally, John LaMay was killed in March. Following Kearney's 25 confessions, 18 murder charges were filed.

During this mayhem, nobody noticed anything odd about Kearney. His supervisor at Hughes Aircraft referred to him as a 'model worker'. However, a local hardware store owner noticed that he kept buying butcher's knives.

HOPING FOR A QUICK CONVICTION

So what happened to John LaMay? When he arrived at Kearney's apartment, Hill was not in. Kearney invited LaMay to stay until Hill returned. While he was watching TV, Kearney shot him in the back of the head. After he had sodomized and dismembered the body, he dumped the remains in the desert. Other missing bodies also seem to have been disposed of there.

'Things disappear very rapidly in the desert,' he said. 'You can put a small animal on an ant hill and it disappears right in front of your eyes.'

However, this made little sense if you dumped body parts in sealed trash bags.

In the end, Kearney was caught due to his own carelessness, but he had had a few close calls earlier. Once, he had a flat tyre and found the spare tyre was flat, too. He had to call a tow truck to get his car to the service station where a new tyre was fitted. The whole time a victim's remains sat on the back seat.

On another occasion, he had got out to inspect a dump site and locked his keys in the car. It took him hours to open the door using a wire coat hanger. Afterwards, however, he felt an even greater sense of relief and empowerment.

Kearney took full responsibility for the murders. He said that all the killings had taken place while Hill was away and he knew nothing about them. After hearing three hours of evidence, the Riverside County Grand Jury refused to indict David Hill. The district attorney admitted that the evidence against Hill was weak and probably not sufficient to take him to court. But the publicity surrounding the case was such that he had to be smuggled out of jail and moved back to Lubbock, Texas.

Kearney's attorney advised him to plead not guilty by reason of insanity. Instead, he pleaded guilty to the first three charges and asked to be sentenced immediately as California was about to reintroduce the death penalty. He was sentenced to life, but with the possibility of parole in just seven years.

'This defendant has certainly perpetrated a series of ghastly and grisly crimes,' said Judge Breckenridge. 'I can only hope the community release board will never release Mr Kearney. He appears to be an insult to humanity.'

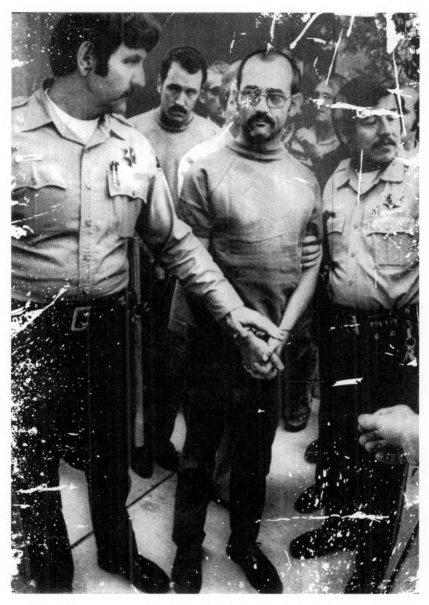

Patrick Kearney, with David Hill behind him (centre) – Kearney took full responsibility for the murders.

There were more hearings. While he seems to have committed around 32 murders, he was charged with only 21 of them. Convicted in every case, he was given a life sentence for each of them. Seven of his victims remained unidentified.

WANETA HOYT

A Mother's Fatal Embrace

MRS WANETA HOYT SEEMED to have been the unluckiest of mothers. Five of her children died of sudden infant death syndrome (SIDS), also known as cot or crib death. This is a catchall term for the unexplained death of an infant. However, in the 1960s and 1970s, there were attempts to discover the causes and give the syndrome some medical credibility.

Waneta Nixon was born in Richford, New York, in 1946. At 11, she caught measles which left her with poor eyesight, only seeing shadows without her glasses. At 17, she married Tim Hoyt, who worked as a Pinkerton guard at Cornell University's art museum 32 km (20 miles) away at Ithaca.

After nine months she gave birth to a son named Eric. He died three months later, on 26 January 1965. The following year she gave birth to James. Their daughter Julie was born in 1968. She died after seven weeks. James was two years old when he died suddenly, too. A grief-stricken Waneta sought help from a psychiatrist, but quit attending after five months.

Three months later, the Hoyts filled out an application at the county's social service agency to adopt a child. But that summer Waneta fell pregnant again and dropped her plans to adopt.

The following March their daughter Molly was born. Fearing that she might also succumb to cot death, the Hoyts took her to the Upstate Medical Center to see Dr Alfred Steinschneider, an expert on sleep apnoea – that is, the sudden cessation of breathing thought to be the cause of SIDS. Molly Hoyt became the first baby in the United States to be sent home on an apnoea monitor. But after just two days, Waneta called Dr Steinschneider because Molly had experienced another spell and she'd had to resuscitate her. Steinschneider told her to bring Molly back to Upstate Medical Center and he readmitted the child. Soon, Molly was discharged and sent home again with the apnoea monitor. The following day, she died. She was two-and-a-half months old.

A week later, the Hoyts made another application to adopt, but this fell through when the caseworker discovered that Waneta was pregnant again. Their fifth child, Noah, was born on 9 May 1971. He was also admitted to the Upstate Medical Center for evaluation. After a month he was discharged. Within three days, Noah was back at Upstate Medical Center. Waneta said Noah had stopped breathing and she'd had to resuscitate him.

On 27 July 1971, he was discharged again. He died the following day. He was two-and-a-half months old. Meanwhile, Tim Hoyt had undergone a vasectomy, thinking that whatever was killing their children was hereditary, so they should not have any more.

A week after Noah died, the Hoyts applied to adopt a child again. On 19 November 1971, they took home a nine-month-old baby boy named Scottie on a six-month trial basis. After five days, Waneta went to see a psychiatrist, fearing that she might hurt Scottie. The psychiatrist suggested to Waneta that she admit herself into a hospital. She refused. Instead, the psychiatrist reluctantly prescribed the drugs Stelazine to treat anxiety and Elavil to relieve depression. The following day, Waneta called social services and asked them to come and pick up Scottie, saying she wanted to wait a year or two before adopting. She then became suicidal.

In October 1972 Dr Steinschneider published a controversial article in the journal *Pediatrics* proposing a connection between sleep apnoea and SIDS. It was based on a case study of a family that had suffered five cot deaths. This seemed to indicate an hereditary cause for sleep apnoea and SIDS. In line with common practice in academic publishing in the medical field, the family were referred to only by their initial H.

Waneta had a hysterectomy in 1973. Then it seems she was raped by a neighbour, though strangely she wanted to continue the relationship with the man. He refused.

The Hoyts finally adopted a two-month-old boy named Jay on 20 September 1976, this time successfully. It was another ten years before Waneta went to see a psychiatrist again, saying that Jay was getting on her nerves. She was supposed to return in two weeks for a second appointment but never showed up.

In 1985, a New York State prosecutor William Fitzpatrick was working on a murder case that had originally been diagnosed as SIDS and consulted Dr Linda Norton, a forensic pathologist from Dallas and an expert on SIDS. In the course of their conversation, Norton remarked: 'You know, you have a serial killer right there in Syracuse.'

She had read Dr Steinschneider's article and told Fitzpatrick the odds against five such cot deaths in one family were incalculably high. She also found it suspicious that the mother was always alone with the babies when they died.

Shortly afterwards, Fitzpatrick left the prosecutor's office, but in 1992 he was sworn in as district attorney and looked into the case again. He consulted forensic pathologist Dr Michael Baden, who concluded that the children had been murdered.

'They were all healthy children,' says Baden. 'They had no natural cause for death. The only reasonable cause is homicidal suffocation.'

Fitzpatrick began tracking down the H family and quickly found that the Hoyts fitted the bill to a T. Noah had been given an autopsy, so Fitzpatrick subpoenaed his medical records from the Upstate Medical Center.

'Several hundred sheets of paper came in, chronicling the life history of this young lad, Noah Hoyt. It was really so sad,' he said. 'For some reason, I developed an emotional attachment to Noah, you know, reading a record of virtually every day in his life. He was going to end up like the other four babies. You wanted to just reach back in through the hands of time and protect him.'

He had breathing problems and sometimes turned blue. There was a similar pattern surrounding the deaths of the other children.

'They all happened while the child was in the exclusive control of the mother,' he noted.

Fitzpatrick was DA in Onondaga County. The Hoyts had moved to nearby Tioga County, so Fitzpatrick contacted the prosecutor there and the state police were called in. They investigated the Hoyts and found they had a clean record. For more than 25 years, each Memorial Day, Waneta would drive to the small cemetery beside her childhood home in Richford to lay flowers on the graves of her babies.

In March 1994, New York State Trooper Bobby Bleck approached Waneta in the post office and asked her if she would help him in some research he was doing on SIDS. She agreed and accompanied him to the police station where she was questioned by three state troopers. Several observers, including Fitzpatrick, watched through a two-way mirror.

At first, she seemed unruffled when they reprised the details of the tragic deaths of her five children years earlier and continued to protest her innocence. Then after an hour, investigator Susan Mulvey took Waneta's hand and said they did not believe her. Fifteen minutes later she admitted killing all five of them.

'I didn't want them to die,' she told the police. 'I wanted them to quieten down.'

Of Eric's death, she said: 'He was crying at the time and I wanted him to stop. I held a pillow – it might have been a sofa throw pillow –

Asked about the fate of her children, Waneta Hoyt insisted: 'I didn't want want them to die. I wanted them to quieten down.'

over his face while I was sitting on the couch. I don't remember if he struggled or not, but he did bleed from the mouth and nose.'

Asked about Julie, she said: 'I held her nose and mouth into my shoulder until she stopped struggling.'

Of James, who was upset about his sister's death, she said: 'I was in the bathroom getting dressed and he wanted to come in. He came in... and I made him go out. He started crying, "Mommy, mommy." I wanted him to stop crying for me so I used a bath towel to smother him.'

Then there was Molly: 'She was just home from the hospital overnight and was crying in her crib. I used a pillow that was in the crib to smother her. After she was dead, I called Mom Hoyt [Tim's mother] and Dr Steinschneider.'

Finally, Noah: 'I held a baby pillow over his face until he was dead. I then called for Mom Hoyt and Dr Steinschneider. I remember it was a hot day in July.'

After her confession, she asked to see her husband and told him what she had said. He said he did not believe her and accused the police of putting words in her mouth. That was not so, she said. He told her he loved her and she continued to tell all to the police.

In her signed statement, she said she had seen counsellors and a psychiatrist.

'I feel that if I had got help from them, it would have prevented me from killing the rest of my children,' she said. 'I feel that I am a good person, but I know that I did wrong. I loved my children. I love my adopted son, Jay, and my husband. I feel the burden I have carried by keeping the secret of killing my children has been a tremendous punishment. I most definitely feel remorse and regret for my actions. I cannot go back and undo the wrong that I have done.'

Waneta Hoyt later recanted her confession and its validity was contested during her trial. Testifying for the defence, Dr Charles Ewing said: 'It is my conclusion that her statement to the police on that day was not made knowingly, and it was not made voluntarily.'

He diagnosed that Waneta Hoyt had dependent and avoidant personality disorders, and was particularly vulnerable to the tactics used during her interrogation. Dr David Barry, a psychiatrist hired by the prosecution, agreed that Hoyt had been manipulated by the police tactics. There was also speculation that she suffered from Munchausen syndrome by proxy, a diagnosis not universally accepted in this case.

Four nurses testified at the trial, saying that Mrs Hoyt showed little interest in her babies.

'There was no bonding at all,' said Thelma Schneider. 'Most of us went to Dr Steinschneider and expressed our fears – we had a gut feeling that something was going on. Either he was in total denial or not being very objective.'

Ambulance worker Robert Vanek, who went to the Hoyt residence when Julie, James and Noah died, recalled being stunned by the coroner's conclusion that all had died of SIDS.

'I thought, three in a row? It bothered me,' he said.

Discounting the post-mortem diagnoses of SIDS, Baden said the children's bodies were examined not by dispassionate forensic pathologists but by the family physician.

'Doctors,' he said, 'don't want to think parents harm children.'

In his testimony Dr Steinschneider continued to insist that the last two children to die suffered severe episodes of apnoea causing the SIDS that he believed had killed them. However, in his 1972 article, he had also noted the Hoyts' emotional detachment.

'Both parents often would be found sitting by the crib and had to be urged to make physical contact with the baby. It was my impression that they feared becoming too attached emotionally... because they anticipated a tragic outcome,' he wrote.

At the end of the four-week trial, Tioga County prosecutor Robert Simpson said in his closing arguments: 'Five young people aren't here today because of her. They would have had families, jobs. But they don't get that opportunity because their mother couldn't stand their crying.'

Waneta's husband Tim stuck by her, saying that the police had twisted her description of the children's deaths to make it sound like a confession. They had worn her down.

'She was used like an old tyre,' he said.

Her adopted son Jay added: 'I love her, and she shouldn't be here. The system sucks.' She, too, remained adamant in court.

'God forgive all of you who done this to me,' she said. 'I didn't kill my babies. I never did nothing in my life, and now to have this happen?' She was convicted of all five murders. Handing down his sentence, Judge Vincent Sgueglia said: 'I only have one thing to say to you and that is to consider your sixth child.... Whatever you tell this court, your husband, your God, you owe it to that boy to tell him the truth.'

On 11 September 1995, she was sentenced to 75 years to life – 15 years for each murder, to be served consecutively – for what Judge Sgueglia described as a 'depraved indifference to human life'. As four deputies escorted her from the courtroom, Jay bowed his head and cried.

Observing Hoyt, aged beyond her 49 years, Fitzpatrick said: 'Despite the cruelty of her acts, you'd be less than human not to have some degree of sympathy for her.'

He was less than sympathetic towards Dr Steinschneider, though.

'How could a doctor not realize that Molly and Noah were in harm's way?' he said. 'I know it was two-and-a-half decades ago. But was he overly consumed with expounding on his theory or was he concerned with his patient?'

Waneta Hoyt died of pancreatic cancer in prison on 13 August 1998. She was formally exonerated under New York law because she died before her appeal could be heard.

INDEX

INDEX

INDEX

INDEX